VIRGINIA WOOLF'S LIGHTHOUSE:
A STUDY IN CRITICAL METHOD

By the same Author

*

THE VOICE OF TRAGEDY
Robert Speller & Sons, New York

VIRGINIA WOOLF'S LIGHTHOUSE

A STUDY IN CRITICAL METHOD

———◆———

Mitchell A. Leaska

1970
COLUMBIA UNIVERSITY PRESS
NEW YORK

Published in England by
The Hogarth Press Ltd
40 William IV Street
London W.C.2
and
in the United States of America by
Columbia University Press
440 West 110th Street
New York, New York 10025

SBN: 231–03403–2

Library of Congress Catalog
Card Number: 77–91807

Printed in Great Britain by
Butler & Tanner Ltd, Frome and London

To
Louise M. Rosenblatt

Acknowledgements

First I should like to thank Mr Leonard Woolf and Virginia Woolf's American publisher, Harcourt, Brace & World, Inc., for granting me permission to quote passages of substantial length from Mrs Woolf's writings. I want also to thank the critics and publishers from whose works brief quotations appear in this text, as specifically acknowledged in the reference notes.

I am grateful to Professors Louise Antz and Joy Gould Boyum for assisting me in the clearer formulation of my own critical views; to Mrs Sarah Willis for her meticulous help with the numerous technical problems in the stylistic analyses; to Mrs Anna Battista for reading and encouraging throughout my revisions; to Mrs Carolyn Heilbrun for her discerning analysis and criticism of the manuscript; to Mr Harry Segessman of Columbia University Press for his constant good faith; and to Mr Leonard Woolf and Professor Quentin Bell for the security of their approval.

Finally, I acknowledge my greatest debt to my teacher and friend, Professor Louise M. Rosenblatt, who first suggested that I make such a study, who refused throughout its course to give me the benefit of a single doubt, but who gave in its stead so generously of her critical acumen and wide scholarship. It was from her remarkable book, *Literature as Exploration*, that I began fully to realize the meaning of the literary experience.

M.A.L.

New York University
September 8, 1968

CONTENTS

7

CONTENTS

FOREWORD

IN recent years there has been a considerable and increasing number of critical works, exploratory or explanatory, about Virginia Woolf's books, particularly the novels. This is mainly due to two reasons. First, although in Britain and other European countries and in America, 27 years after her death, she is widely treated as one of the most important writers of her time, there is considerable difference of opinion regarding her stature as a novelist. Secondly, after *The Voyage Out* and *Night and Day*, beginning with *Jacob's Room*, she broke away from the traditional form and method of the English novel and developed a highly individual technique, which culminated in *The Waves* and *Between the Acts*. The technique, structure, form, content, and meaning of these later novels are extremely complex, and much of the labour of the critics has been devoted to unravelling the complexity and explaining the intention and meaning of the novelist. Here too the wide differences in understanding and interpretation are remarkable.

Mr Leaska's analysis and interpretation of *To the Lighthouse*, to which I have been asked to write this foreword, are the most illuminating study of Virginia Woolf's novels which I have read—indeed, the only work comparable with it for critical illumination is the monumental study by Professor Guiguet. A foreword should be extremely short and should stand only for a brief minute between the reader and the author, and I will therefore only deal with a few points. Mr Leaska insists upon the importance of Virginia Woolf's method which he calls 'manifold perspectives' or 'multiple points of view'. The kernel of her novels is not a story, a plot of action; it is a number of people, their relations to one another and to the fundamentals of life, to life itself, to love, to art, to death. The

9

method is to present events, the characters of the *dramatis personae*, their thoughts, relations to one another and life and death and the universe, their past and their present, not through a single eye of God or of the novelist or of an 'I' in the novel itself, but through both the omniscient writer and the characters in the novel one after the other, a multiple-point-of-view which gives the manifold perspective. This method produces 'the delicate art of exploring human experience and human associations'; and thus in *To the Lighthouse* 'the whole constellation of emotional and mental processes which make up human experience is revealed to the reader'.

The reader must read the book for himself in order to find out whether he thinks these claims are substantiated. There are only two other points I wish to make. The difference of opinions with regard to the meaning and value of Virginia Woolf's novels among professional critics is, as I have said, very great, some rating some of the books as masterpieces and others rating all of them as negligible. This does not surprise me, since between 20 and 30 years after a writer's death there is very often a violent ebb and flow in his reputation. What has always surprised me is the extraordinary difference of opinion regarding (to put it crudely) what the novels are about. The hostile critics usually maintain that the novels are about nothing, having no story or plot, the persons being unreal persons without real characters, and in so far as they do exist, being highly sophisticated, precious cardboard figures solely concerned with the superficial, hothouse or drawing room relations of a snobbish clique. Now I am not here concerned with the judgment of value, i.e. whether the novels are good or bad novels artistically, whether they succeed or fail. I am concerned solely with the question: what are they about? The moment one asks that question, the judgment of the hostile critics seems extraordinary. It seems to me impossible to read *To the Lighthouse* and not see that, beneath the surface of events and the kaleidoscope of thoughts and dialogue, the subject of the book, the pivot of the novel, is the most important and complex relations of human beings and the most profound problems of human existence; and that, further, the characters of the *dramatis personae* are not simplified cardboard, but extremely subtle and complicated. The great merit of Mr Leaska's analysis is that he gives an extremely original and convincing exposition of how this is achieved in the novel.

Finally, many professional critics maintain or assume that the novels, because of their esoteric artificiality or preciosity, are not understood or appreciated by the common reader, and are now what is called 'out of date'. For instance, one well-known critic has said that *To the Lighthouse* is not read by the ordinary person, because it is ununderstandable to the common reader today in a way which *Tristram Shandy* was not ununderstandable to the common reader of Sterne's day. I will give some facts which, I think, allow one to conclude inductively that this view is mistaken; it also seems to me that Mr Leaska's analysis gives one *a priori* reasons for believing that the ordinary reader, once he became accustomed to Virginia Woolf's method, would find no difficulty in understanding and appreciating *To the Lighthouse*. There are facts of two kinds to support this conclusion. The novel was published 41 years ago and its author died 27 years ago. Yet I am continually getting letters from ordinary men and women telling me of the profound effect of her books, and particularly *To the Lighthouse*, has had upon them. To show exactly what this means, I will quote from a letter received by me on August 5th, 1968, from an entirely unknown person, a woman teacher:

It is with considerable trepidation that I write to you thus for I know that my letter must be one of so many similar; nevertheless I am urged on by my deep affection for the writing of your wife, Virginia Woolf. . . . Time has never before allowed me to indulge wholeheartedly in her writing; now that I have begun to do so it is difficult to explain how

FOREWORD

deeply her books have affected me, and, through them a personality which I seem to have been seeking all my life.

It is also said from time to time that the novels have fallen out of fashion and favour and are now read by very few. The sales of Virginia Woolf's books show that this is not true. The sales of *To the Lighthouse* in each of the last three years in Britain and the United States have been as follows:

	Britain	USA	Total
1965	21,991	21,309	43,300
1966	22,100	30,860	52,960
1967	30,873	25,780	56,653

The student of literary reputation in the contemporary world will be interested to study the following figures:

Sales of *To the Lighthouse* in the first three years and the last three years of publication:

	Britain	USA	Total
1927–1929	4,412	7,261	11,673
1965–1967	74,964	77,949	152,913

LEONARD WOOLF

Monk's House
Rodmell, Lewes, Sussex
18 August 1968

Chapter One

INTRODUCTION

THE writer of fiction who relinquishes the privilege of addressing his reader directly, who chooses to present his story dramatically through various angles of perspective imposes upon himself many restrictions. Virginia Woolf is one such author of what is called the subjective, multiple-point-of-view novel. For over four decades her work has elicited considerable critical commentary. But despite the many studies dealing with her modes of narration, her technical devices, her use of language, and so on—most of which attempt to explain the means by which she has handled her self-imposed restrictions—no single study analyses in detail the rhetorical effects of shifting points of view together with an objective analysis of the stylistics associated with each of those points of view. And these are precisely the areas I have undertaken to examine and elucidate in this essay.

In a preliminary effort with college students, this multiple viewpoint-stylistic approach to several of Mrs Woolf's novels has proved to be successful, particularly with the individual uninitiated in the ways of psychological realism. For one thing, the reader is not only made aware of who the narrator is but also learns to determine what kind of narrator he is; and as a result the reader is better able to evaluate the quality and the reliability of the material being presented to him. Secondly, his being made alert to the manner in which narrators are shifted as well as to the shift itself, provide him with a deeper understanding of thematic synthesis and artistic design. He becomes increasingly aware, moreover, of how Mrs

Woolf has overcome the limitations imposed by the impersonal mode of narration.

Therefore, inasmuch as this investigation deals with critical theory, my primary concern was towards systematically working out a detailed and realistic critical method which could be applied to other novels and which would, in addition, encourage other students of fiction to enlarge upon and refine further the present system of analysis by applying it to earlier novelists and to those yet to come.

The need for such a method became apparent while surveying the critical literature dealing specifically with the novel taken up in this study. Numerous misjudgments of character and misinterpretations of thematic material seemed to have their source in the commentators' lack of awareness of the significance both of the points of view and of the sequence in which they appear in the work. Moreover, there were critics who clearly betrayed their inability to distinguish between one narrator and another even in the face of what appeared to be quite obvious differences in tone and style. Much critical confusion has resulted from these misreadings.

Many entries in the bibliography contain partial studies of novelists whose works have become part of the aesthetic ethos of western culture and suggest, as well, possible future investigations dealing with the rhetoric of point of view and the stylistic devices associated with it. Just how, technically, these works have charmed some readers and perplexed others for generations seems a worthwhile contribution to practical criticism and to critical theory in general.

Studies related to the present investigation fall generally under the headings of: point of view as a critical concept and as a technical device; style in literature (some dealing specifically with Virginia Woolf); and studies of literary criticism and language. The appended bibliography is in some measure qualitatively selective and contains a number of entries which have only an indirect bearing on the present study. However, because their applicability has been the informing principle, they will be important to anyone who intends to explore rhetorical and stylistic analysis of prose fiction.

In literary criticism the concept of point of view is a very old one, spanning nearly twenty-five hundred years. At one extreme stands Plato, who, in *The Republic* (Book III), made the distinction between 'simple narration' and 'imitation'. Using a passage from Homer, he illustrated how the poet's voice was affected by changing direct discourse into indirect; that is, how imitation could be 'translated' into narration. With dialogue as his main concern, he spoke of drama as most nearly approaching the pure imitative style because the poet's voice had disappeared entirely.

At the other extreme stands James Joyce, who, through Stephen Dedalus in *A Portrait of the Artist as a Young Man* (middle of Chapter V), distinguishes between the lyric and the dramatic forms: 'The personality of the artist, at first a cry or cadence or a mood (lyric) . . . finally refines itself out of existence (drama), impersonalizes itself. . . .'

Less than a decade later (1921), with Henry James' critical prefaces as his basis, Percy Lubbock coherently formulated in theory the problem of point of view. He saw two distinct novel forms: the *dramatic*, in which the story acts itself out before the reader in much the same manner as does a play; and the *panoramic* or *pictorial*, the method in which an author narrates his story to the reader. In their essential outline, the statements of Plato, Joyce, and Lubbock are concerned with the same fundamental relationship.

Critics and practitioners of fiction have given much energy to the problem of point of view. Their discussions have been instructive in that, among other things, it is possible to see that the concept of point of view provides a critical tool, an operational mode, for determining the degree to which the author has 'removed' himself from the narrative itself. The implications of this authorial presence or reticence will be considered at length in the discussion of the rhetoric inherent in impersonal narration and its relation to literary effects.

Norman Friedman's essay, 'Point of View in Fiction: The Development of a Critical Concept',[1] sketches the aesthetic background of the concept and outlines its emergence as an instrument for criticism. General though the study is, its discussion of the significance of the focus of narration in relation to artistic technique is indeed impressive; it is also suggestive of the kinds of study open to the student of fiction.

In *The Rhetoric of Fiction* (1961), Wayne C. Booth made a large-scale study of the complex problems the writer faces when he attempts to impose his fictional world upon the reader. With references, varying in amount and detail, to over a hundred works of fiction, Booth examined the rhetorical dimension of literature in terms of the vast range of technical resources available to the author in his effort to help the reader grasp the work. The study is extremely valuable not only because Booth convincingly repudiates a number of arbitrary assumptions, which have long since contaminated critical theory—such as the distinction between the purity of form and the morality of content; but also, and more important, because the study raises many significant questions which force us to examine more scrupulously the rhetorical means by which the fusion of form and content is effected for the reader.

A preliminary study of the entries found in the extensive bibliographies of both Friedman and Booth indicated that the definitions of point of view found in most glossaries of literary terms are inadequate and often misleading. Since, in addition to the reader's intellectual and emotional involvement, his moral judgments play a significant role in determining how much of the fictional world he will accept, such questions as a narrator's reliability, for example, were considered to be as significant as whether the narration was given in the first person or in the third, or whether the narrator was omniscient or limited.

A survey of these discussions revealed, moreover, that the focus of narration is not only a problem which is *fundamental* to any communication between author and reader but also an invaluable critical tool when it is considered a technical device. As Mark Schorer writes in 'Technique as Discovery'[2]: 'Technique is the only means the writer has of discovering, exploring, developing his subject, of conveying its meaning, and finally, of evaluating it.' In these terms, point of view becomes a technical device susceptible to study by the critic concerned with exploring the problem a writer faces in presenting his object *while simultaneously evaluating it*. The degree to which he makes his evaluation clear to the reader reflects, ultimately, the success with which the author's rhetoric has transformed a private vision into something essentially public.

As the bibliography indicates, there are numerous general studies of style and stylistics as well as those dealing with the style and technique of particular writers. These studies offered many useful suggestions both for developing a methodology and for providing a general frame of reference necessary for this kind of investigation. Richard M. Ohmann's study, *Shaw: The Style and the Man* (1962), for example, is an impressive analysis of the author's style by the methods of the new linguistics. In his essay, 'Prolegomena to Prose Style',[3] Ohmann very convincingly sets forth the idea that style is not just a *way* of saying *something*; he contends rather that it is a matter of epistemic choice which reveals a writer's mode of experience; that is, the linguistic choices a writer makes shows 'how he imposes order on the ephemeral pandemonium of experience'.[4] And when Leo Spitzer says that 'language is only one outward crystallization of the "inward form",[5] he is speaking of that inner unifying principle which exists in a writer —a kind of emotional consistency which is observable in his linguistic habits. Spitzer's analysis of Diderot's prose style[6] bears eloquent testimony to this contention and demonstrates as well the sensitivity of a critic who *sees style as part of the meaning*. His thesis, in a sense, recalls John Middleton Murry's statement that 'a true idiosyncrasy of style is the result of an author's success in compelling language to conform to his mode of experience';[7] and it is very likely what Wimsatt refers to in his study of Samuel Johnson when he says that style is the 'last and most detailed elaboration of meaning'.[8]

Out of the Conference on Style (Indiana University, 1958) came *Style in Language*,[9] a publication made up of papers presented by scholars in the fields of linguistics, psychology, cultural anthropology, and literary criticism. Although the work offered little in the way of specific material for this study, it was helpful in pointing out and evaluating alternatives of methodological procedure. In addition, relationships between the disciplines of literary criticism, linguistics, and psychology were made clearer, and many methods of analysis also were examined—such as the statistical and the linguistic—methods often not amenable to problems of poetics. In light of these discussions, it became more obvious that such approaches to literary analysis as outlined by Edith Rickert,[10] although interesting and suggestive, by themselves, remain, ultimately, just that. Scientific in its approach as literary criticism strives to be and helpful as codifiers and computers are, the critic, it seems to me, must finally strive to be his own most reliable instrument; and as such he must constantly be alert to test himself against possible sources of error.

Other related critical discussions either deal briefly with many, or in detail with few, aspects of technique and style; or deal in detail with the problems inherent in choosing the focus of narration. But so far as I can discover, no single study offers a systematic or comprehensive method of analysis for determining how the manipulation of, and the stylistics associated with, multiple points of view function rhetorically to clarify the meaning of a work.

Inasmuch as I. A. Richards is largely responsible for having laid down the foundations of contemporary literary criticism, his continually influential *Principles of Literary Criticism* (1930)[11] was consulted to clarify certain of the more troublesome aspects of the critical process. Other studies such as Wellek and Warren's *Theory of Literature* (1949) and Herbert Read's *The Nature of Literature* (1956) have been extremely helpful in explaining the nature of criticism and in formulating the assumptions on which the study of literature is conducted. Of the more specific variety, such studies as Mark H. Abrams' *The Mirror and the Lamp* (1958) have been useful not only in demonstrating critical methodology—no less impressive than that found in William Empson's *Seven Types of Ambiguity* (1955)—but also in illuminating the subtle relationship between criticism and the creative sensibility.

Although without direct relationship to literary criticism, such studies in language as S. I. Hayakawa's *Language in Thought and Action* (1949) and Roger Brown's *Words and Things* (1958) were considerably useful in clarifying how a writer's linguistic virtuosity orders the experiences and attitudes of his reader. Equally important for the more complex problems in semantics and symbolism were such studies as *Science and Sanity: An Introduction to Non-Aristotelean Systems and General Semantics* (1948) by Alfred Korzybski and *The Meaning of Meaning* (1946) by C. K. Ogden and I. A. Richards.

Chapter Two

AN IDEA OF THE METHOD

SOME readers may never have the creative or intuitive equipment to distinguish between one point of view and another. One of the principal reasons, I think, is that often these readers lack sufficient insight into the author's language to make distinctions in the tone of the various narrators. A novelist such as Virginia Woolf, for instance, requires of her reader what a playwright requires of an actor: namely, to read the verbal symbols, the words and phrases themselves, appropriately so that their emotional suggestiveness and coloration may be felt.

Anyone who has had the misfortune to attend a play-reading given by inexperienced actors will sense immediately that their main difficulty is in their inability to convey or to modulate the tone; that is, to capture some of the feelings the dramatist experienced when he was creating his *personae*. Similarly, some readers of the novel are unable to grasp the implicit evaluation which the author has concealed behind the words of his narrator's explicit statements.

In a multiple-point-of-view novel such as Virginia Woolf's *The Waves*, for example, the formal divisions of the narrative are clearly indicated, and the problem of identifying a narrator does not ordinarily present itself. But in a work such as *To the Lighthouse*, determining the angle of narration requires special attention, because the sharp line between narrator and character, between one character and another, or between the author and narrator has dissolved. In this manifold stream-of-consciousness novel, there may be as many as four or five shifts of point of view within a single sentence; and precisely where the shift occurs is often not easy to determine. Moreover, there are occasional passages which are presented simultaneously from more than one point of view—that is, the passage may be shared simultaneously by two or more of the narrators; or the material may be presented in such a way as to make it impossible to distinguish between the omniscient narrator and the perceiving consciousness of a character.

The problem, then, of determining the various points of view was approached by watching carefully for specific indications of a shift from one angle of perspective to another. The explicit statement of a narrator was perhaps the simplest index of a shift; it was also the tone of, or the feeling implicit in, the statement that identified a particular consciousness. It was necessary, therefore, to attend to such things as syntactical peculiarities: the introductory clause, the participial phrase, the mood and tense of the verb, the repetition of a particular word or phrase, the conditional sentence, and so on. All of these and other devices as well were found to be inconspicuous but important signals for directing the reader from one consciousness to another.

It is true that even an experienced critic may mistake a narrator or the tone of his utterances, because the author has made or has left the passage ambiguous. The confusion over Swift's position in relation to Gulliver's in the fourth book of *Gulliver's Travels* is an excellent example of an ambiguity of tone. The author, however, is the cause of error only some of the time.

It is true also that a reader need not go through all this detective work to get through the novel. But if he learns some of the techniques for determining the narrator, the tone, the feeling, et cetera, his literary experience will be enlarged considerably; and he will also be more sensitive to the subjective novel as well as to the subtleties of other kinds of imaginative literature.

The problem of studying a multiple-point-of-view novel is complicated by the fact that very often the narrators, through whose minds the fictional material is being filtered, are not established for us at the beginning of the work, but rather are given to us piecemeal, elusively; so that even at the end, though we may see a narrator in his entirety, we do not necessarily see him conclusively: he remains the sum of our impressions, a fluid personality.

The method of creating each narrator is, in a sense, additive; and our impression of him grows as his reflections and impressions and utterances accumulate. Thus our understanding of him is also, in a sense, additive, since what we know of him is actually a synthesis of our accumulated impressions.

Therefore, to study systematically *To the Lighthouse* as a model of the multiple-point-of-view novel, it was necessary first to isolate, then consolidate, analyse, and interpret the content of the material — that is, the reflections on, the impressions of, and the utterances about events and people — given by each narrator, independent of and untempered by the thoughts and utterances made by other narrators. By this process, the personality and character of a particular narrator was essentially being deduced, as a spectator might deduce the personality of an individual in whose consciousness he is trapped.

It was from this kind of separation and isolation — artificial as it necessarily is — that made it possible to glean the progression of a narrator's mental activity, in all its depth and variety, which communicates that 'semi-transparent envelope' which surrounds his essence as a human personality. And because that personality is a principal thread in the fabric and meaning of a manifold-consciousness novel, by analysing it, as outlined above, it was also possible to assess and finally to assemble each narrator's experience of one another and of the world outside.

Moreover, since literature is by nature temporal, it was possible to examine the manipulation of viewpoints — the larger dimension of rhetoric — by considering the sequence in which the various angles of perspective were introduced. Operationally, this part of the investigation was carried out by noting both the order in which the narrators appeared and the amount of information given each time; and by ascertaining from the material, whether the information moved the story forward by filling in hiatuses; whether it corrected what had been given previously; whether it disagreed with what preceded— keeping the story 'suspended' while simultaneously adding one more reflecting surface; or whether the information prepared (or 'warned') the reader for the narrator who was to follow.

Inasmuch as the author makes the meaning of his story available to the reader by his choice of narrator(s), it was possible, from the data collected, to make some generalizations as to (1) how *what* was said, through each of the multiple points of view, and (2) how the *order* in which it was said, controlled the reader's detachment or sympathy and guided his intellectual, emotional, and moral progress through a fictional world of values.

In the final part of the study, my primary aim was to see, by close textual analysis, what stylistic characteristics, if any, differentiate the narrators. For there is no longer any doubt that an individual's linguistic habits project his personality. More than two decades ago, F. H. Sanford wrote:

> There are many indications that language is a vehicle of personality as well as thought, for when the person speaks, he tells us not only about the world but also, through both form and content, about himself.[1]

And as was indicated earlier, the reader is very often made aware of a shift in point of view by the narrator's explicit statement.

But since linguistic changes at times also indicate a shift in the focus of narration, the samples, for the stylistic analysis of each point of view, were taken from sections as early in the text as that narrator first appeared and provided material in which no (or as few as possible) interruptions were introduced by intervening narrators.

For each Woolf narrator, the sample is exactly 840 words in length (or 7560 words for the entire novel). That particular figure was determined by the fact that the utterances of one narrator (Mrs McNab) do not exceed that number; therefore all of the samples were reduced to that figure for the sake of consistency and also because it made working with raw values possible, which meant that statistical normalization—and sometimes distortion—was not necessary.

The length of the samples was determined on the basis of other stylistic investigations which seemed to me, in various ways, related to this one. For example, under the supervision of Edith Rickert, one of the pioneer researchers on stylistic analysis, one study was made at the University of Chicago by Josephine M. Lane (*An Analysis of the Style of Dorothy Richardson's Novels*). In her analysis, J. M. Lane selected one chapter from each of Miss Richardson's novels—chapters ranging in length from 575 to 2100 words (with the mean length: approximately 1340 words per novel).

Another systematic piece of research was Richard M. Ohmann's recent study of George Bernard Shaw's style, a doctoral investigation conducted originally under the direction of Professors Harry Levin and Reuben Brower of Harvard University. In the published version of the study, Ohmann wrote that '2600 words is easily a large enough sample to reveal the style of an author'.[2]

John B. Carroll's research project, 'Vectors of Prose Style',[3] sponsored by the United States Office of Education, was conducted with samples of various sources and styles of prose not much more than 300 words in length. Moreover, using the dimensions he had identified in his study, Carroll demonstrated, again with 300-word samples, the stylistic differences between the writing of F. Scott Fitzgerald and that of Mickey Spillane.

Judging from these studies, I felt that the length of the samples used was justified on several counts: first, this part of the investigation was not made to discover the style *of the author*, but rather to see if there are stylistic differences *between the narrators*. Second, the purpose was to look at the way Mrs Woolf handled the problem of authorial 'silence'. Third, since the work here focuses only on the stylistic features which help the reader to distinguish between narrators, I avoided making any statistical generalizations about the total body of a narrator's utterances. And last, inasmuch as this part of the study was an effort to supplement the critical judgments of the earlier section (Chapter Five), the work is not to be construed as a statistical study, as such.

Each of the samples has been analysed for sentence structure (particularly clause embedding), vocabulary, verb density, personal affect, ornamentation, abstract nouns, and imagery—with each item clearly defined in each of the discussions. All comparisons have been phrased in terms of individual differences between the various narrators in the novel; that is, they could not be compared with anything else. Since each novel is a self-contained universe and the narrators, its population, there is nothing with which to compare the values except with each other.

While the computer is extremely helpful, accurate, and time saving, it could not be used in this section of the investigation except for processing some of the data; and the reasons, I think, are obvious: in the identification of clause types, for example, since there are no *specific* verbal cues which consistently *differentiate* one type from another, the computer can be of no assistance. Nor can it distinguish between images and mental pictures or between concrete nouns and those abstract nouns which are used concretely—or those concrete nouns which have both abstract and concrete components. More important, since verbal structures may be classified in several ways depending on their position and function, at the present time only the human intelligence is capable of making those decisions on classification. And lastly, as John B. Carroll summed it up: 'Although the style of literary passages can be indexed in certain ways mechanically, it cannot be *evaluated* mechanically!'[4]

Both qualitative and quantitative methods were employed, as appropriateness dictated. When some dimension of the author's style was not readily mensurable either because it appeared too infrequently or because that dimension was so merged in the whole texture of the work that it could not be counted with any degree of accuracy, as with the imagery, for example, then it was analysed and interpreted descriptively. 'There is,' as F. H. Sanford wrote

> . . . a reasonable argument, reinforced by some empirical evidence, that a quantitative analysis of written expression can discover individuality. It may well be, however, that there are subtle aspects of uniqueness in style which cannot be uncovered by analytical procedures. It is reasonable to expect that the sensitive observer can appreciate relationships and coexistences which escape objective analysis. The brain is a more subtle instrument than the calculating machine.[5]

The close textual analysis in this study has been limited to Virginia Woolf's *To the Lighthouse*, because it represents a major (and very difficult) multiple-point-of-view work of a major British novelist. There are two other specific reasons for the Woolf selection: the first is that the angles of narration are not clearly marked, nor are the shifts clearly indicated; and secondly, *To the Lighthouse* employs a larger number of points of view than either *The Waves* or *Mrs Dalloway*.

Another prominent English subjective novelist, Dorothy Richardson, was mentioned only in passing here because her vast pioneer novel, *Pilgrimage*, is limited to the single focus of narration of Miriam Henderson. Similarly, James Joyce has been given only minimal space, because his monumental work, *Ulysses*, has already been investigated with regard to style and technique.

Although Virginia Woolf has been of central concern

in developing this critical approach to the multiple-point-of-view novel, other writers such as Henry James, Gustave Flaubert, Joseph Conrad, Ernest Hemingway, D. H. Lawrence, and William Faulkner have been considered whenever their mention seemed appropriate for clarifying a point or making some comparison or contrast.

Finally, since critics have dealt with the problem of authorial silence mainly in contemporary fiction, historical antecedents and influences have, for the most part, been left unexamined. Moreover, because this study deals, in the broadest sense, with technique and style as rhetoric, a consideration of the numerous social and psychological forces that come to life in any transaction between author and reader has, of necessity, been minimized — as has been the tendency towards philosophical speculation.

Chapter Three

THE CONCEPT OF POINT OF VIEW

THE question of who shall narrate the story or through whose eyes the reader shall see is one which every writer of the novel has had to face. The question does not seem to have been an especially vexing one to novelists of the past. But since the beginning of the modern novel — more specifically, since Henry James — with a more vigorous determination to achieve a greater reality of both the inner and the outer life to reveal the whole of experience, the choice of the angle or angles of narration, through which the story is to be transmitted, has created a great deal of difficulty and concern among literary craftsmen, artists, and critics alike.

In his critical prefaces, now collected as *The Art of the Novel* (1934), James was deeply concerned with problems of literary method, particularly the method of narrative presentation through a single consciousness — the 'central intelligence' or the 'sentient centre' or the 'reflector', as he variously called it. Drawing principally from James' prefaces, Percy Lubbock, in *The Craft of Fiction* (1921), coherently formulated James' concepts about point of view — concepts which, since Lubbock, have become fairly rigid and consequently transmuted, by later critics of fiction, to a somewhat dogmatic statement of theory.

Wayne C. Booth, however, in his study, *The Rhetoric of Fiction* (1961), in re-examining these earlier critical interpretations of method and procedure, has, by carefully pointing out weaknesses and fallacies in the doctrine, made perhaps the most significant single attempt at revising and modifying so important a concept as point of view. This critical evolution notwithstanding, however, it is important to recognize that as pioneer in and practioner of the theory of point of view, Henry James was an advance guard of the new psychological fiction.

As every storyteller knows, a tale conceived in a particular way has certain affective potentialities over a reader's feelings and attitudes. But just how that tale is presented to the reader will determine whether those affective potentialities either become vivid or remain lifeless on the page. A useful way of considering point of view as a technical problem is to think of a novelist presenting his story as if he were a motion-picture director filming a script. The question to arise first is what angle or what combinations and variations of angles of vision will most effectively project the story for the viewer. After settling this question, the director must decide when to move the camera up close and when to increase the distance between the viewer and the viewed; when to reveal a scene slowly and when to quicken the pace; how to effect transitions smoothly from one angle to another so as to create a sense of continuity; whether to unfold the story chronologically or scramble the sequence while simultaneously building up a sense of relatedness and integration. All of these, and many more, are problems which must be dealt with if the story is to be transmitted intelligibly, vividly, and—most important—persuasively. The choices made will be determined, ultimately, by the choice of the angle or angles of vision.

Generally, for the novelist there are three broad possibilities open. The first of these is the point of view of the *omniscient narrator*. According to Beckson and Ganz, the omniscient view

> enables the writer to present the inner thoughts and feelings of his characters. Godlike, he may survey from his Olympian position past and present so that the reader may come to

know more of his imaginative world than any single character in it. In *Ulysses*, for example, a work that employs shifting points of view, Joyce reveals the inner thoughts of his three major characters through the stream of consciousness . . . and presents actions, unknown to the individual characters, going on in various parts of Dublin. Moreover, the omniscient author may sometimes openly comment on the behavior of his characters, as in Thackeray's *Vanity Fair*. . . . [1]

In omniscient narration, the author tells the story *after* it has happened. Moreover, the omniscient narrator may borrow, at will, the point of view of any of one or another character and observe things from that person's angle of perspective; and he may, with authorial responsibility, at other times, choose to abridge some part of the story, or comment on it, or take a panoramic view of it.

The opening lines from three different novels will illustrate the general tenor of omniscient narration:

from Hardy's *The Mayor of Casterbridge:*

> One evening of late summer, before the present century had reached its thirteenth year, a young man and woman, the latter carrying a child, were approaching the large village of Weydon-Priors, in Upper Wessex, on foot. They were plainly but not ill clad, though the thick hoar of dust which had accumulated on their shoes and garments from an obviously long journey lent a disadvantageous shabbiness to their appearance just now.

from Jane Austen's *Pride and Prejudice:*

> It is a truth universally acknowledged that a single man in possession of a good fortune must be in want of a wife.
> However little known the feelings or views of such a man may be on his first entering a neighbourhood, this truth is so well fixed in the minds of the surrounding families, that he is considered as the rightful property of some one or other of their daughters.

THE CONCEPT OF POINT OF VIEW

from Tolstoy's *Anna Karenina:*

> Happy families are all alike; every unhappy family is
> unhappy in its own way.[2]

One of the distinguishing features of an omniscient
narrator is his power not only to inform the reader of the
ideas and emotions of his characters, but also to reveal, in
varying degrees, his own biases, whether by overt authorial
intrusions or by the way in which he generalizes about
life, morals, manners, and so on. This method of narration
may very often be editorial in attitude; that is, the author
not only reports ideas and events, but he criticizes and
passes judgments on them as well.

I have been describing the omniscient narrator as
primarily *telling* the story rather than dramatizing it. And
in so far as *telling* is concerned, I have tried to emphasize
the fact that summary narrative (as this mode of telling is
often called) is characterized, in part, by the general
manner in which events are reported; by the indefinite
period of time such events cover; by the variety and freedom of locations where such events occur; by the tendency
of the author-narrator to editorialize, to criticize, and,
openly, even to judge.

The omniscient narrator, however, with all the latitude
of storytelling he assumes, may choose to *dramatize*, to
show the reader rather than to tell him. The method is
theatrical, 'objectified', as it were. When the omniscient
narrator chooses to have his characters—no one of their
consciousnesses, now, open to view—act and speak
equally before the reader, the authorial voice becomes neu-
tral, the point of view impersonal, detached—'detached',
that is, *only as it is possible in any work of fiction.*

When the author subdues his own vociferous presence,
he, in a sense, forces the reader to deduce, from all the
details he has seen and heard, his own generalizations as
to what is going on and what his own attitude should be
towards the spectacle placed before him. Because the

31

reader, if he is to respond appropriately, requires from the scene the transmission of considerable data, one natural consequence of the stratagem is the presentation of a *specific* temporal and spatial framework capable of containing the concrete details and enclosing the dialogue—all of which are the *sine qua non* of the dramatic mode.

Because Flaubert favoured this impersonal stance of omniscient narrator, two scenes from *Madame Bovary* will serve to illustrate—the first, primarily dialogue; the second, primarily detail:

> He took her hand, and this time she did not withdraw it.
> 'First prize for all-round farming!' cried the chairman.
> 'Just this morning, for example, when I came to your house . . .'
> 'To Monsieur Bizet, of Quincampoix.'
> 'Did I have any idea that I'd be coming with you to the show?'
> 'Seventy francs!'
> 'A hundred times I was on the point of leaving, and yet I followed you and stayed with you . . .'
> 'For the best manures.'
> '. . . as I'd stay with you tonight, tomorrow, every day, all my life!'
> 'To Monsieur Caron, of Argueil, a gold medal!'
> 'Never have I been so utterly charmed by anyone . . .'
> 'To Monsieur Bain, of Givry-Saint-Martin!'
> '. . . so that I'll carry the memory of you with me . . .'
> 'For a merino ram . . .'
> 'Whereas you'll forget me; I'll vanish like a shadow.'
> 'To Monsieur Belot, of Notre-Dame . . .'
> 'No, though! Tell me it isn't so! Tell me I'll have a place in your thoughts, in your life!'
> 'Hogs: a tie! To Messieurs Leherisse and Cullembourg, sixty francs!'
> Rodolphe squeezed her hand, and he felt it all warm and trembling in his, like a captive dove that longs to fly away;

but then, whether in an effort to free it, or in response to his pressure, she moved her fingers.

'Oh! Thank God! You don't repulse me! How sweet, how kind! I'm yours; you know that now! Let me see you! Let me look at you!'

A gust of wind coming in the windows ruffled the cloth on the table; and down in the square all the tall head-dresses of the peasant women rose up like fluttering white butterfly wings.

(Part 2, Chapter 8.)

But it was above all at mealtime that she could bear it no longer—in that small ground-floor room with its smoking stove, its squeaking door, its sweating walls and its damp floor tiles. All the bitterness of life seemed to be served up to her on her plate; and the steam rising from the boiled meat brought gusts of revulsion from the depths of her soul. Charles was a slow eater; she would nibble a few hazel-nuts, or lean on her elbow and draw lines on the oilcloth with the point of her table knife.

(Part 1, Chapter 9.)[3]

One important rhetorical function effected by the dramatic mode is to persuade the reader that he sees and ultimately judges for himself. This, in itself, has a great deal of appeal for the reader because a sense of immediacy has been achieved. It follows that if *showing*, unattended by authorial commentary and overt direction, effects a sense of immediacy, then one further difference between the narrative method and the dramatic is that in the narrative the distance between the story and the reader is considerably greater than it is in the dramatic, in which the very effect of impersonal presentation creates a more personal involvement of the reader with the story.

Suffice it to say, that in omniscient narration, the author has many advantages of dealing with both the story and the character in various descriptive and developmental ways. But one salient characteristic prevails with omniscient narration: namely, the author's readiness to place himself between the reader and the story to clarify a point, to make a confident interpretation of what otherwise might remain ambiguous and bothersome, and so on. And while no twentieth-century reader should be disturbed when something is made clear for him, if he is sufficiently conscious of some of the subtleties which obtain in all omniscience, he may become more alert as a reader when he begins to realize that even when the author is presenting something dramatically, he renders the scene through his own eyes rather than through the eyes of his characters—thus creating, however tenuous, a mediatory distance between the reader and the story.

The evolution towards direct presentation in the novel marks the chain of events in the course of which the novelist relinquishes some of his possible points of view; and by so doing, he also surrenders many sources of information which were available to him as an omniscient author. As he deprives himself of the privilege of commentary when he resorts to presenting his story dramatically, so the author denies himself any direct pronouncements in his fictional proceedings when he bequeaths his tale to a narrator who is either an observer or a participant in the story.

If the novelist chooses as his narrator a *first-person observer*, he restricts himself to some extent in that the narrator, as the observer, no longer has access to the inner states of the characters involved and, therefore, can report only what he witnessed or has genuinely discovered or, in extreme cases, has drawn inferences from. He may even guess. But he is not allowed entry into the minds of the principal characters of his story. The narrator-observer, moreover, although he views the story from what Friedman calls the 'wandering periphery',[4] like the omniscient narrator, is given the prerogative of presenting his material at any given point either as summary narrative or as scene. Thus the distances or variations in distance established between the reader and the story will, for the most part, be determined by the narrator's choice and manipulation of his modes of presentation—that is, whether by the narrative mode or the dramatic.

Because the narrator-observer, in reporting his story, is simultaneously interpreting that story, the reader's response to it and to his interpretation of it will inevitably be influenced by the impression he gets of the narrator, himself. It is necessary, therefore, to notice how, either before introducing the narrator or by endowing him with special self-evident characteristics such as honesty, perceptiveness, et cetera, the author persuades the reader that the narrator is worthy of his attention and trust.

Joseph Conrad in *Heart of Darkness*, for example, prepares us for Marlow's tale:

> . . . The yarns of seamen have a direct simplicity, the whole meaning of which lies within the shell of a cracked nut. But Marlow was not typical (if his propensity to spin yarns be excepted), and to him the meaning of an episode was not inside like a kernel but outside, enveloping the tale which brought it out only as a glow brings out a haze, in the likeness of one of these misty halos that sometimes are made visible by the spectral illumination of moonshine.

When there is no preparation, when the reader has no way of knowing about the narrator except from the process of his 'acting himself out', there is apt to be trouble. One of Henry James's least popular novels, *The Sacred Fount*, is a good example. The story is an account of a weekend party at a place called Newmarch; and it is told by an unnamed narrator who spends his entire time there trying to fathom the relationships between some of the guests. Very early in the novel, we learn that he sees close human relationships as a depletion of one individual for the enrichment of the other—metaphorically, as a 'sacred fount' being drained.

From the very beginning, the reader is trapped in the

consciousness of the narrator: there is no prelude or introductory information about him given from some other source. As a result, the reader is to the very end helplessly confined to only the evidence which the narrator chooses to furnish. And since he makes no bid for our sympathy in his rather unengaging search for depleted characters, we are at a loss as to how credible a witness he is. It takes no profound analysis to discover that the narrator is given to flights of fantasy; that he keeps a good deal of emotional distance between himself and others; that his drive for intellectual superiority is compulsive; and that he is obsessed with the notion that he is capable of 'reading into mere human things an interest so much deeper than mere human things were in general prepared to supply'. In fact, he reports what other characters in the story say of him: 'You're abused by a fine fancy'; 'You over-estimate the penetration of others'; '. . . people have such a notion of what you embroider on things that they're rather afraid to commit themselves or to lead you on'; and so on.

The reader, if he has managed to maintain enough interest to finish the novel, discovers at the end that nothing has been solved; in fact, nothing has actually happened that needs to be solved except for evaluating the narrator's ornate and highly suspect ruminations. Perhaps one of the surest pleasures to be derived from the work, either by the student of James or by the psychological critic, is in deducing the character and personality of an extremely complex and ambiguous narrator, because in this short novel James has pushed the impersonal aspect of the point-of-view method almost to the limits of absurdity. It is, therefore, small wonder that *The Sacred Fount* has never found either a wide or an enthusiastic reading public.

The long shelf of fiction is filled with stories told by *first-person narrator-participants*; that is, by narrators who have been actively involved in the events and reported, in their own voice, the story from a point in time *after* the experience itself. Moll Flanders, Huckleberry Finn, Jane

Eyre, Claudius, Holden Caulfield, David Copperfield
mention only a few of these narrators who are also principal participants in the stories they tell. Quite often these
narrators speak in the first-person voice, because that
voice gives an impression of being livelier and more direct;
and confidence can be more quickly established than with
the use of the third-person voice.

When the 'I' is used, however, the author denies himself more channels of information. More than that, he must
surrender some of the vantage points the narrator-
observer enjoyed from his 'wandering periphery'. Now the
narrator-participant is centrally involved in the action,
with his angle of perspective fixed at the centre of the
experience he relates. In so far as concerns the source of
his information, he is limited to his own thoughts, feelings,
and perceptions. As Moll Flanders, for example, says very
early in her 'History and Misfortunes':

> This is too near the first hours of my life for me to relate
> anything of myself but by hearsay; 'tis enough to mention
> that, as I was born in such an unhappy place, I had no
> parish to have recourse to for my nourishment in my in-
> fancy; nor can I give the least account how I was kept alive,
> other than that, as I have been told, some relation of my
> mother took me away, but at whose expense, or by whose
> direction, I know nothing at all of it.

In subtler pieces of fiction however, the limitations set
on available information are convincingly overcome by a
narrator's capacity to speculate and to draw inferences.
For example, Conrad works around the problem in the
opening pages of *The Secret Sharer*:

> On my right hand there were lines of fishing stakes *re-*
> *sembling* a *mysterious* system of half-submerged bamboo
> fences, *incomprehensible* in its division of the domain of
> tropical fishes, and *crazy* of aspect *as if* abandoned forever.
> . . . To the left a group of barren islets, *suggesting* ruins of
> stone walls, . . . *There must have been* some glare in the
> air. . . .[5]

But the narrator-participant angle of view can offer problems to the reader. For one of the liveliest debates in contemporary criticism, we need only look at the conflicting interpretations given to the governess' story in James' *The Turn of the Screw*. The problem arises, among other things, from the fact not only that James has kept her impersonal, to the extent of leaving her unnamed — very much the same as the narrator in *The Sacred Fount* — but also that the reader's introduction to her by Douglas, the outer and indeed very favourable frame of reference, tends to cast her in a most auspicious light — a setting in which we are prepared even before meeting her to accept as absolute truth her testimony of the ghastly happenings at Bly.

But when readers' opinions of the governess range from that of a sexually repressed psychotic to that of an 'honourable and fearless lady', as Rebecca West thinks of her, it is no longer a question of a reader's alertness or stupidity: it is rather more an issue of James' having willfully obscured his narrator-participant ('lucid reflector' seems inappropriate in this instance). The result is that few of us, as Booth remarks, 'feel happy with a situation in which we cannot decide whether the subject is two evil children as seen by a naïve but well-meaning governess or two innocent children as seen by a hysterical, destructive governess'.[6]

It is ironic that of all novelists, it was Henry James who, in a letter to H. G. Wells, concerning the dangers of first-person narration, called it that 'accursed autobiographic form which puts a premium on the loose, the impoverished, the cheap and the easy. Save in the fantastic and the romantic . . . it has no authority, no persuasive or convincing force. . . .'

Although thus far I have dealt exclusively with first-person narrator-observers and participants, a narrator — whether an observer or a participant — is employed very often, and as effectively, with the *third-person* voice. The method of narrator-observer, with no 'I' to alert the reader that an experiencing mind is mediating between him and the event, is a subtle device which frequently causes the inexperienced reader to think that the fictional material is coming to him directly. Even though the author may give his narrator no personal characteristics, there are certainly effects which are produced by the undramatized narrator's tonal characteristics and the attitude he projects towards what he is reporting.

In this method of narration, everything depends directly on the presentation of background, external action, gesture, and speech. Since the method tends to transmit the story as a dramatic presentation of objectives scenes, a sense of detachment and impersonality may be created. It shares, moreover, one basic limitation with the first-person narrator-observer: namely, that it does not permit of any direct account of the inner states of the characters under observation except in terms of surmise.

Because Hemingway creates perhaps the most rigorously impersonal stories by means of the undramatized narrator, the following passage from his short story, 'Soldier's Home', will serve to illustrate:

> . . . He had tried so to keep his life from being complicated. Still, none of it had touched him. He had felt sorry for his mother and she had made him lie. He would go to Kansas City and get a job and she would feel all right about it. There would be one more scene maybe before he got away. He would not go down to his father's office. He would miss that one. He wanted his life to go smoothly. It had just gotten going that way. Well, that was all over now, anyway. He would go over to the schoolyard and watch Helen play indoor baseball.

When the *narrator-participant* is rendered in the *third person*, the unsuspecting reader, again, may confuse it with omniscient narration. D. H. Lawrence's *Sons and Lovers*, for example, is frequently thought of as narrated by the author; but if one stopped to consider where the fictional ballast lay, he would soon realize that the story, with the exception of the first three chapters, comes filtered almost entirely through Paul Morel, and it is his story—told in the third-person voice. Perhaps the surest index to discovering the author's choice of vantage point is to consider the character on whom he focuses the reader's attention and on that character's relationship to the action of the story. In the case of the third-person narrator-participant, if the selected character has no relation to a particular event, or if some occurrence is of no interest to him or is beyond his understanding, then no report of it is made.

Henry James' *The Ambassadors* is a worthy example of third-person-participant narration. In his discussion of that novel, Percy Lubbock says that James does not 'tell the story of Strether's mind; he makes it tell itself, he dramatizes it'.[7] He says further that everything in that work is rendered objectively: 'whether it is a page of dialogue or a page of description nobody is addressing us, nobody is reporting his impression to the reader. The impression is enacting itself in the endless series of images that play over the outspread expanse of the man's mind and memory.'[8] Perhaps the most important assertion Lubbock makes in his discussion of this Jamesian novel is that the presentation in time is integral to the objective method, because it requires the reader to 'live' through the experience with the character—and at *his* pace.

Equally significant in the objective method is that it forces the reader to organize the story for himself, to make of it what he will. The French critic, Ramon Fernandez, suggests this aspect when he describes the novel as a 'representation of events which take place in time, a representation submitted to the conditions of apparition and development of these events'.[9]

The third-person-narrator-participant method is particularly effective in *The Ambassadors* not only because the reader's sympathies are likely to be given up to Strether very early in the work, but also because the full awareness of his desires pitted against the restrictions of his conscience—the internal struggle dramatically depicted in the novel—is a conflict known to everyone at one time or another. *The Ambassadors* is, moreover, a perfect example of James' success in the fusion of form and content, because as a work of art it is an eloquent testimony of the dictum which occupies the very centre of James' aesthetic of the novel: and that is, to show something intensely, it must be shown from the appropriate angle of vision.

Finally, narrator-observers and participants, whether first person or third, have the privilege, at any given point, of summarizing the narrative or of presenting it dramatically, thereby modulating at will the distance between the reader and the story, by technical means. What is important here (as with omniscient narration) is the fact that distance—which in aesthetic terms is inversely proportional to involvement or sympathy or identification (critical terminology is inadequate on this point)—is ultimately the result of the author's or the narrator's or the character's effect on the reader. It makes no difference whether the voice is 'I' or 'he' or 'she' or 'we'. The intellectual and moral and emotional qualities of the narrator, in the last analysis, will be more important in molding a reader's experience and judgment than the person of the voice. Our delight with Moll Flanders, our disapproval of Wickham in *Pride and Prejudice*, our pity for Anna Karenina, our disgust with Kafka's country doctor, our aversion to Faulkner's Jason Compson should indicate that the achievement of a literary effect has no fast or fixed rubric.

So long as there is a narrator, someone is mediating between the reader and the story. The next step in the direction of objectification is effected by doing away with the narrator altogether and dramatizing the inner state of a *persona* by *direct mental transmission*; that is, by confronting the reader directly with the mental experience of a character. One vivid example which illustrates direct transmission is found in James Joyce's *A Portrait of the Artist as a Young Man:*

... When would he be like the fellows in Poetry and Rhetoric? They had big voices and big boots and they studied trigonometry. That was very far away. First came the vacation and then the next term and then again the vacation. It was like a train going in and out of tunnels and that was like the boys eating in the refectory when you opened and closed the flaps of the ears. Term, vacation; tunnel, out; noise, stop. How far away it was! It was better to go to bed to sleep. Only prayers in the chapel and then bed.

(Chapter I)

So thoroughly has Joyce given us the novel in terms of Stephen Dedalus, and so purged is the text of his own authorial presence, that readers coming to the work for the first time accept the fictional material to the extent that they frequently find themselves making only those value judgments which are shared by the narrator himself: for example, they share the profound seriousness with which he views himself; they accept the somewhat debauched version of aesthetic theory he offers; and they marvel, as much as Stephen himself, at his own artistry.[10]

When the mental atmospheres of two or more *personae* are presented, we have what might be called *multiple inner points of view*. The method of presentation—similar to that of a single consciousness—is almost entirely in the direction of scene, both of an inner view of the mind and of an outer view by means of speech and action. Erich Auerbach calls the method the 'multipersonal representation of consciousness'[11] and points out that one of the possibilities of the multiple-consciousness method is its 'obscuring and even obliterating the impression of an objective reality completely known to the author'.[12] Discussing a passage from Virginia Woolf's *To the Lighthouse*, Professor Auerbach observes that Mrs Woolf

42

presents herself 'to be someone who doubts, wonders, hesitates, as though the truth about her characters were not better known to her than it is to them or to the reader'.[13] The statement is extremely significant in that it has to do not only with the author's attitude towards reality, but also, and more important, with the relationship between the form of the novel and how that form defines and communicates its meaning. This aspect will be discussed later in considerable detail.

In the multiple-point-of-view method, when a descriptive detail is necessary, it is supplied by way of 'stage direction', as Norman Friedman calls it, or it is given through the thoughts and utterances of the *personae* themselves.

When the novelist maintains the third-person angle throughout, as does Virginia Woolf, in both *Mrs Dalloway* and *To the Lighthouse*, one might legitimately ask how precisely this differs from an omniscient-author-point-of-view novel. The difference, though often not susceptible to detection, is chiefly this: While in the omniscient-author-point-of-view novel, the author looks into the minds of his characters and relates to the reader what is going on there, the information is presented as *he* sees and interprets it, rather than as his people see it. Moreover, in the traditional omniscient novel, the information is narrated as though it had already occurred. In the multiple-point-of-view novel (as I shall refer to it hereafter), however, the mental contents—the thoughts, feelings, and perceptions of the *persona*—are rendered as they seem and feel to him. In addition, the mental states are presented scenically as if the settings or situations which evoked those states were happening *now* before the reader, at the time of the reading. In brief, life is presented as it seems to the fictional people who are living it. As a consequence, the physical appearance of a character, what he does, what he thinks and feels—in short, all the fictional data—are communicated through the consciousness of someone present.

A passage from *To the Lighthouse* followed by a 'translation'[14] of that passage will point out precisely the difference:

> He was really, Lily Briscoe thought, in spite of his eyes, but then look at his nose, look at his hands, the most uncharming human being she had ever met. Then why did she mind what he said? Women can't write, women can't paint—what did that matter coming from him, since clearly it was not true to him but for some reason helpful to him, and that was why he said it? Why did her whole being bow, like corn under a wind, and erect itself again from this abasement only with a great and rather painful effort? She must make it once more. There's the sprig on the tablecloth; there's my painting; I must move the tree to the middle; that matters—nothing else. Could she not hold fast to that, she asked herself, and not lose her temper, and not argue; and if she wanted revenge take it by laughing at him?

It is possible to rewrite this passage, now, as an omniscient author would by shifting to indirect discourse, by normalizing the grammar and syntax, by changing all the personal pronouns to the third person, and by rearranging slightly the thoughts to create the impression of the logical sequence which characterizes public discourse:

> Looking at his nose and hands, Lily Briscoe thought that he, in spite of his eyes, was the most uncharming human being that she had ever met. She did not know why she minded his saying that women could not paint or write. She knew that it did not matter coming from him, since clearly he did not believe it. And she wondered if he said it because, for some reason, it was helpful to him. Yet she could not understand why her whole being bowed, like corn under a wind, and only with great and rather painful effort, erected itself again from the abasement. She knew that she must make it once more. She looked at the sprig on the tablecloth and thought of her painting; she knew that she would

have to move the tree to the middle. To her, only her painting mattered—nothing else. That was why she questioned
if she could hold fast to that and not lose her temper and
argue. She wondered why, if she wanted revenge, she did not
take it merely by laughing at him.

One major problem of the multiple-point-of-view novel
is determining the consciousness presenting the material
at any given point. Not every novel of this type, however,
offers that difficulty. In Faulkner's *As I Lay Dying*, for
example, each shift of point of view is indicated by the
narrator's name immediately before his section. In another
of his novels, *The Sound and the Fury*, despite whatever
other problems the text may offer, identifying the *persona*
is not one of them. Faulkner here marks off the four major
divisions of the novel by different dates; and he indicates
the change of *persona* by establishing conspicuous differences in the images and ideas of each as well as in the
language in which they are expressed.

The rigorous formality of Virginia Woolf's *The Waves*
similarly offers no special difficulty in so far as identifying
the speaking voice is concerned. The novel—it is perhaps
more appropriate to refer to it as a poetic drama—is
broadly designed in scenic arrangements which correspond
progressively to the rising and setting of the sun and to
the flooding and ebbing of the tides. The progress of the
sun and tide symbolically marks the growth of the six
characters in the work—Bernard, Neville, Louis, Susan,
Jinny, and Rhoda. Each scene, prefaced by a brief
passage of lyrical prose, presents a set of highly stylized
soliloquies, the ideas, images, and language of which run
parallel in growth and maturity to the progress of the day,
the activity of the tide, and the position of the waves on
shore. And although the *personae* characteristically speak
with the impeccable vocabulary and in the fastidious
style of their author there is no ambiguity about who
is speaking, because Mrs Woolf throughout identifies

each *persona* with 'said Bernard', 'said Rhoda', et cetera. Moreover, even if the 'he said' device had not been employed, the reader might still easily identify the character by sensing the singular powers of perception with which each is peculiarly endowed. Even as children, the special gift each possesses is apparent:

'I see a ring,' said Bernard, 'hanging above me. It quivers and hangs in a loop of light.'

'I see a slab of pale yellow,' said Susan, 'spreading away until it meets a purple stripe.'

'I hear a sound,' said Rhoda, 'cheep, chirp; cheep, chirp; going up and down.'

'I see a globe,' said Neville, 'hanging down in a drop against the enormous flanks of some hill.'

'I see a crimson tassel,' said Jinny, 'twisted with gold threads.'

'I hear something stamping,' said Louis. 'A great beast's foot is chained. It stamps, and stamps.'

(Part I)

Because *To the Lighthouse* is a less formal and more complex novel than *The Waves*, the reader is confronted with the problems of how Virginia Woolf manipulates manifold points of view; on what the difficulties are in distinguishing between the viewpoints; and of how Mrs Woolf does, in fact, provide signals for identifying the principal narrators.

Chapter Four

MULTIPLE VIEWPOINTS
IN 'TO THE LIGHTHOUSE'

THE problem of determining the variations and combinations of point of view in Virginia Woolf's *To the Lighthouse* is apparent in the first six sentences of the novel which demonstrate the subtlety with which Mrs Woolf manipulates her manifold points of view while simultaneously modulating their tone.

(1) 'Yes, of course, if it's fine tomorrow,' said Mrs Ramsay. (2) 'But you'll have to be up with the lark,' she added.
(3) To her son these words conveyed an extraordinary joy, as if it were settled, the expedition were bound to take place, and the wonder to which he had looked forward, for years and years it seemed, was, after a night's darkness and a day's sail, within touch. (4) Since he belonged, even at the age of six, to that great clan which cannot keep this feeling separate from that, but must let future prospects, with their joys and sorrows, cloud what is actually at hand, since to such people even in earliest childhood any turn in the wheel of sensation has the power to crystallize and transfix the moment upon which its gloom or radiance rests, James Ramsay, sitting on the floor cutting out pictures from the illustrated catalogue of the Army and Navy Stores, endowed the picture of a refrigerator, as his mother spoke, with heavenly bliss. (5) It was fringed with joy. (6) The wheelbarrow, the lawnmower, the sound of poplar trees, leaves whitening before rain, rooks cawing, brooms knocking, dresses rustling—all these were so coloured and distinguished in his mind that he had already his private code,

47

his secret language, though he appeared the image of stark and uncompromising severity, with his high forehead and his fierce blue eyes, impeccably candid and pure, frowning slightly at the sight of human frailty, so that his mother, watching him guide his scissors neatly round the refrigerator, imagined him all red and ermine on the Bench or directing a stern and momentous enterprise in some crisis of public affairs.

The first two sentences are, of course, spoken by Mrs Ramsay. In the third sentence, however, 'To her son these words conveyed an extraordinary joy . . .', we move into the young boy's mind; without any discernible change in syntax or vocabulary, we are shifted into the mind, and are being given a brief inside view, of the boy who had so looked forward to this expedition 'for years and years it seemed'—for who other than for this young boy would it have *seemed* like 'years and years'? The fourth (and the short fifth) sentence belongs clearly to the Omniscient Narrator: the sudden expansiveness of the ideas, the auctorial command with which they are presented, and the shift to the present tense all indicate the presence of the all-seeing, all-knowing, objective angle of perspective. The sixth sentence begins again with James's feelings— 'all these were so coloured and distinguished in his mind that he had already his private code, his secret language, though he appeared . . .'—and shifts for the first time into Mrs Ramsay's thoughts with 'though he appeared . . .'. We see James, now, through her eyes and share her feelings for her son as she watches him cutting out pictures from an illustrated catalogue.

The example here demonstrates several of the ways in which to determine who is narrating. However, it also suggests the angle from which, as well as the manner in which, the material is being given. This kind of awareness is extremely important in Mrs Woolf's novel because the lines separating narrator and author, and narrator and character, are, in most cases, very obscure. In some instances, therefore, it is vital to see, to 'feel', the various ways the author places the narrator, since the position the reader feels will often establish for him the narrator's location in the setting; and this not only firmly identifies him but also clarifies his relationship to the action. More significantly, the reader's ability to sense the narrator's coign of vantage will ultimately help him to determine the narrator's function in defining part of the over-all pattern and meaning of the work.

When James, for example, feels his extraordinary joy at the prospect of the expedition, his position is central. The very fact that it is *his* feeling places him in the centre of the scene. When the Omniscient Narrator moves in, however, a change of position is felt, because we are no longer experiencing the intimacy which resulted from our having an inside view of James and thus sharing his feeling of joy. The Omniscient Narrator now presents and explains not only James but people in general who belong

> to that great clan which cannot keep this feeling separate from that, but must let future prospects, with their joys and sorrows, cloud what is actually at hand, since to such people even in earliest childhood any turn in the wheel of sensation has the power to crystallize and transfix the moment upon which its gloom or radiance rests. . . .

This material presented omnisciently is characterized chiefly by its indefiniteness in time and place, its generalized statements about people and life, its expanded detail, and its unlimited perspective. And it is precisely because of these characteristics—all of them impersonal to varying degrees—that the distance increases between the story and the reader because the narrator seems removed to some Olympian height when presenting his material.

A closer and more systematic examination of the novel reveals some of the reasons why it is difficult for some Woolf readers to distinguish the various angles of perspective. In the first place, the language itself of all the *personae* seems to be characteristically that of Virginia Woolf. Because she does not, like Joyce in *Ulysses*, go to the deepest levels of the characters' consciousnesses, the reader is not given those linguistic configurations of pre-speech utterance—that is, utterances having no resemblance to those of public discourse—which are likely to differentiate one individual from another. In the second place, because her method of presenting the contents of her characters' minds is, according to Robert Humphrey's classification, primarily indirect interior monologue,[1] her own language very often becomes subtly fused with the language of her characters. Thirdly, because of the resulting linguistic similarity, it is difficult—sometimes impossible, even after the closest analysis—to tell precisely when a character's consciousness ceases to be represented and that of the Omniscient Narrator takes over. Fourth, once Mrs Woolf has introduced the reader to the character's mind and given him sufficient feeling for the way that mind works, for them to proceed comfortably together, she removes herself from the scene; the moment she leaves, however, the interior monologue changes immediately from indirect to direct. Finally, because the points of view shift so often and the direct and indirect interior monologue alternate so frequently—all of this executed with extraordinary perfection and subtlety—the reader, if he is at all aware of the techniques operating before him, may become thoroughly baffled when he attempts to separate one voice from another. Let us examine a typical passage (the numeration is added for analytical convenience):[2]

(1) 'It is a triumph,' said Mr Bankes, (2) laying his knife down for a moment. (3) He had eaten attentively. (4) It was rich; it was tender. It was perfectly cooked. (5) How did she manage these things in the depths of the country? he asked her. (6) She was a wonderful woman. (7) All his love, all his reverence, had returned; (8) and she knew it.

(9) 'It is a French receipe of my grandmother's,' said Mrs Ramsay, (10) speaking with a ring of great pleasure in her voice. (11) Of course it was French. (12) What passes for cookery in England is an abomination (they agreed). (13) It is putting cabbages in water. It is roasting meat until it is like leather. It is cutting off the delicious skins of vegetables. (14) 'In which,' said Mr Bankes, 'all the virtue of the vegetable is contained.' (15) And the waste, said Mrs Ramsay. A whole French family could live on what an English cook throws away. (16) Spurred on by her sense that (17) William's affection had come back to her, and that everything was right again, and that her suspense was over, and that now she was free both to triumph and to mock, (18) she laughed, she gesticulated, (19) till Lily thought, (20) How childlike, how absurd she was, sitting up there with all her beauty opened again in her, talking about the skins of vegetables. (21) There was something frightening about her. She was irresistible. (22) Always she got her own way in the end, Lily thought (151–52).

The first sentence is traditional enough in that at (1) the words are reported, and at (2) a 'stage direction' is given omnisciently. At (3) however, without any announcement, we are given Mrs Ramsay's thought: we can be certain of it here, because we know that she wishes to please Bankes and is, therefore, concerned with the attention he has given the food. At (4) the three short statements, now with the tense shifted from past perfect to imperfect, we continue in Mrs Ramsay's mind, now with even greater immediacy, because they are presented as pure direct interior monologue. At (5) the interior monologue changes to direct statement, with quotation marks omitted; but at (6) we are again presented, by direct interior monologue, Mr Bankes' thought—a thought which presumably he would never utter aloud. At (7) we are again sharing *directly* with Mrs Ramsay her pleasure in having succeeded in pleasing Bankes; and at (8), by way of confirmation, the Omniscient Narrator concludes the paragraph. Although the content of (7) would not seem to warrant it, it might be argued that (8) is presented as indirect interior monologue. But there is no way of being absolutely certain.

The first sentence of the second paragraph is identical in *form* to the opening sentence of the preceding paragraph: (9) the 'audible' report, followed by (10) the Omniscient Narrator describing and interpreting the tone. The second sentence, (11), is clearly Mr Bankes' thought presented by means of direct interior monologue. The next sentence is likewise his; the '(they agreed)' is simply an economical touch of omniscience. The next three sentences, (13), are also filtered through Bankes' consciousness as evidenced by his manner of enumerating and his attention to detail—both characteristics belonging to a scientist and a food faddist. Further, Mrs Woolf finishes his sentence, a fragment though it is, with the traditional use of quotation marks and so connects (14) with (13) which might remain ambiguous in so far as voice is concerned.[3] The next sentence, (15), though clearly Mrs Ramsay's utterance, appears visually as indirect interior monologue; and neither the content nor the conversational tone would indicate the necessity for Mrs Woolf's ignoring conventional punctuation. In sentence (16) we have an omniscient beginning, shifting at (17) to Mrs Ramsay's thoughts, now by means of indirect interior monologue—as the third-person pronoun, the past perfect and imperfect tenses, and the intimate use of Bankes' first name attest. The two independent clauses in (18) are omniscient statements in one sense. But they are also a very delicate shift towards Lily Briscoe's consciousness, a shift which is completed by (19): 'till Lily thought', after which, the content of her mind is presented through indirect interior monologue at (20), direct interior monologue at (21), and indirect again at (22).

This brief analysis should, I think, indicate the futility of any attempt to make generalizations about determining the angles of narration in this novel. Each page has its own wonders; and in each the opportunities for confusion are legion. And the reader, when he has become aware that shifts of perspective are even occurring, begins to watch for them and gradually becomes sensitive to the effect of the shift, although he may not always be able to point precisely to where it occurred. Rather than generalize then, it seems more useful to enumerate some of the kinds of signals to watch for, and to point out some of the problems which result when the signals are not clear.

The most obvious signal for identifying a narrator is Mrs Woolf's use of the 'he said', 'he thought', device. At times the utterance or the thought is followed by an editorially omniscient 'stage direction'. For example:

'It's due west,' said the atheist Tansley, holding his bony fingers spread so that the wind blew through them . . . (12).

There is a variation of this device, this one considerably more refined. Referring to Mrs Ramsay and Charles Tansley, Mrs Woolf writes in an auctorial statement:

She looked at him.

With no overt direction or narrator signal, the statement is followed immediately by:

He was such a miserable specimen, the children said, all humps and hollows. He couldn't play cricket; he poked; he shuffled. He was a sarcastic brute, Andrew said. They knew what he liked best—to be forever walking up and down, up and down, with Mr Ramsay, and saying who had won this, who had won that . . . (15).

As readers we know only that Mrs Ramsay is looking at Tansley. Yet the content of the passage and the tone of anger and disparagement which permeates it identifies the lines as coming from Mrs Ramsay, as being her impressions of the young man.

The following passage illustrates the occasionally baffling similarity between a narrator's utterance and omniscient-narrator commentary. It demonstrates, however, how punctuation can signal a shift in the angle of perspective. Here Mrs Ramsay is walking with Tansley:

> He should have been a great philosopher, said Mrs Ramsay, as they went down the road to the fishing village, but he had made an unfortunate marriage. Holding her black parasol very erect, and moving with an indescribable air of expectation, as if she were going to meet some one round the corner, she told the story; an affair at Oxford with some girl; an early marriage; poverty; going to India; translating a little poetry 'very beautifully, I believe', willing to teach the boys Persian or Hindustanee, but what really was the use of that?—and then lying, as they saw him, on the lawn (19–20).

The extraordinary subtlety of the shift is located in Virginia Woolf's use of the semicolon after 'story'; had she placed a colon there instead, although the account sounds as though it might be coming from her, the reader might easily be misled to think that the Omniscient Narrator is enumerating, through summary narrative, part of the account of Carmichael which Mrs Ramsay had begun earlier to tell her companion.

The present participial phrase, the interpretive summary statement, and the use of parentheses, all occasionally function to signal an omniscient-narrator intervention. The following scene is between Lily Briscoe and William Bankes (I have italicized the omniscient statements):

> But the number of men who make a definite contribution to anything whatsoever is very small, he said, *pausing by the pear tree, well brushed, scrupulously exact, exquisitely judicial. Suddenly, as if the movement of his hand had released it, the load of her accumulated impressions of him tilted up, and down poured in a ponderous avalanche all she felt about him.*

Here we shift into Lily's consciousness:

> That was one sensation. Then up rose in a fume the essence of his being. That was another. *She felt herself transfixed by the*

intensity of her perception; it was his severity; his goodness. I respect you (*she addressed silently him in person*) in every atom; you are not vain; you are entirely impersonal; you are finer than Mr Ramsay; you are the finest human being that I know; you have neither wife nor child (*without any sexual feeling, she longed to cherish that loneliness*), you live for science. . . .

How then did it work out, all this? How did one judge people, think of them? How did one add up this and that and conclude that it was liking one felt, or disliking? And to those words, what meaning attached, after all? *Standing now, apparently transfixed, by the pear tree, impressions poured in upon her of those two men, and to follow her thought was like following a voice which speaks too quickly to be taken down by one's pencil, and the voice was her own voice saying without prompting undeniable, everlasting, contradictory things, so that even the fissures and humps on the bark of the pear tree were irrevocably fixed there for eternity.* You have greatness, she continued, but Mr Ramsay has none of it (39–40).

The italicized lines are markedly different from Lily's thoughts and utterances; and the 'she continued' in the last lines is further evidence that her interior monologue has been interrupted by the commentary of the Omniscient Narrator.

When the content itself of a narrator's utterance acts as the signal, the character and tone of his words will invariably reinforce the reader's sense of the particular consciousness through which the material is coming. In the example which follows, Mrs Ramsay has just finished questioning her husband's prediction that the morrow's weather would not be fine; and the paragraph which follows, with no *persona* markers whatever, begins:

The extraordinary irrationality of her remark, the folly of women's minds enraged him. He had ridden through the valley of death, been shattered and shivered; and now, she flew in the face of facts, made his children hope what was utterly out of the question, in effect, told lies (50).

Here the material, someone might insist, is being presented omnisciently. But if we examine it carefully, we would find at least three clues indicating Mr Ramsay as its source; namely, the angry impatience, the ready self-indulgence, and the tone of utter exasperation—all of which characterize him and thereby establish him unquestionably as the *persona*.

Occasionally Virginia Woolf presents, simultaneously, feelings shared, simultaneously, by two consciousnesses. In what follows, for example, James and his sister, Cam, are angrily preoccupied with their father's lack of consideration for them:

> Now they would sail on for hours like this, and Mr Ramsay would ask old Macalister a question—about the great storm last winter probably—and old Macalister would answer it, and they would puff their pipes together, and Macalister would take a tarry rope in his fingers, tying and untying some knot, and the boy would fish, and never say a word to anyone (244).

Once more, someone might argue that the Omniscient Narrator is reporting their thoughts and feelings. But again there are at least three clues which tend to contradict that assertion: in the first place, the sentence begins with 'Now', establishing the time as the fictional present which characterizes the contemporaneousness of interior monologue; secondly, the verb auxiliary, 'would', shifts all the verb forms to the subjunctive mood, thereby making all the actions they are thinking about actually contingent upon their father's whim; it indicates, moreover, that they are, possibly without realizing it, conjecturing—which the word, 'probably', would tend to support; third, the whole passage is one sentence consisting of six independent clauses joined by 'and'; and the resulting polysyndeton functions here to suggest the breathlessness of their adolescent impatience and anger. What is especially remarkable is that Mrs Woolf has convincingly created a mutually shared interior monologue with such seeming effortlessness. In fact, she uses 'they' twice in the passage, and intuitively the reader knows that the first 'they', referring to James and Cam, is the pronoun which establishes them as the *personae*. We might also observe, incidentally, how in the next sentence— keeping all the aforementioned elements constant, except for the possessive adjective, 'his', and the personal pronoun, 'he'—Mrs Woolf shifts us now into only James' mind and keeps us there briefly for two sentences, after which we are given more omniscient narration.

Another device the author utilizes to designate a particular narrator is the use of the 'tag' phrase, a phrase which eventually becomes associated with a narrator. When the reader becomes familiar with the narrators, the phrase begins to function as a signal for him, indicating that a shift has taken place as well as making it possible for him to identify the voice. Mrs Ramsay's favourite, 'after all', will illustrate the point (italics have been added to omniscient-narrator statements):

And after all—after all (*here insensibly she drew herself together, physically, the sense of her own beauty becoming, as it did so seldom, present to her*)—after all, she had not generally any difficulty in making people like her; for instance, George Manning; Mr Wallace; famous as they were, they would come to her of an evening, quietly, and talk alone over her fire. *She bore about with her, she could not help knowing it, the torch of her beauty; she carried it erect into any room that she entered;* and after all, veil it as she might, and shrink from the monotony of bearing that it imposed on her, her beauty was apparent. She had been admired. She had been loved (64–65).

Around the first omniscient statement, Mrs Woolf has placed parentheses. Because she has not done so with the other two, they might easily pass unnoticed were it not for the fact that when we are back with Mrs Ramsay's thoughts, we realize that what she is thinking is essentially the same as the omniscient statements; only now the idea is repeated ostensibly in her idiom. And it is precisely here that the phrase, 'after all', takes on semantic significance: given to sympathy-seeking and self-depreciation, Mrs Ramsay recognizes—uses—her beauty as a *last resort*, only; *after all* else has failed to soothe and restore her sense of self, usually following some real or imagined injury—in this case, Carmichael's refusing her offer to get him anything from the village. 'After all', then, is an effective, appropriate, and telling introductory phrase for a woman who, under ordinary circumstances, feels she must 'veil' her beauty and 'shrink from the monotony of bearing that it imposed on her . . . .'

Finally, since the most difficult distinctions in these manifold perspectives occur between the Omniscient Narrator and the various other narrators, it might be well to indicate some of the verbal choices which appear frequently enough in omniscient passages to be considered one of their distinguishing features. Below is a partial listing of excerpts of omniscient statements to which italics have been added:

It was *as if* the water floated off . . . (33).

Suddenly *as if* the movement of his hand had released it . . . (39).

but then, raising his hand, half-way to his face *as if* to avert . . . their gaze, *as if* he begged them to withhold for a moment . . . *as if* he impressed upon them . . . (41).

. . . (and this *must* refer to *some* actual incident) . . . (34).

. . . fishing them up out of her mind by a phrase which, coming back from *some* party . . . (88).

Prue Ramsay died that summer in *some* illness connected with childbirth . . . (199).

it was to pin down *some* thought more exactly . . . (283).

. . . whose virtue *seems* to have been laid bare . . . (38).

. . . the boat *seemed* to drop into this silence, this indifference, this integrity, the thud of *something* falling (201).

. . . (she accomplished here *something* dexterous with her needles) . . . (96).

Quickly, *as if* she were recalled by *something* over there, she turned to her canvas (309).

. . . he bent quizzically and whimsically to tickle James' bare calf with a sprig of *something* . . . (49).

. . . *perhaps* a tear formed; a tear fell . . . (46).

. . . this swoop and fall of the spirit upon truth which delighted, eased, sustained—falsely *perhaps* (46).

. . . it was not him, that old man reading, whom he wanted to kill, but it was the thing that descended on him—without his knowing it *perhaps* . . . (273).

. . . even as they descended, one saw them twisting about to make *Heaven knows what* pattern on the floor of the child's mind . . . (84).

Supposedly, these are omniscient statements; but when we begin to notice the 'seems's, the 'perhaps's, the unspecified 'something's, and so on, we begin to question the narrator's omniscience: we sense him to be a little diffident; a little uneasy—uncertain. As Erich Auerbach observed,[4] he is one, curiously, who doubts; who questions; who hesitates. In this quality of muted dubiousness, he shares at times, with the other *personae*, their attempt to approach and to fathom the mysteries of concrete reality and, ultimately, their quest for truth. And the uncertainty and haziness of vision with which Mrs Woolf, as omniscient author, has endowed her Omniscient Narrator, as we shall see, has considerable meaning in the total significance of the work itself.

We might conclude, then, from this preliminary discussion that the concept of point of view which Henry James set forth and which Percy Lubbock later formulated in theory is possibly one of the most significant approaches to the novel prior to the new generation of critics. The term itself, 'point of view', is important not only because it is general and pliant and therefore avoids the kind of problem in literary taxonomy which confronts the reader of Edwin Muir and the follower of Northrop Frye; but also because the term applies fundamentally to the relation in which the novelist stands to his story. And if part of what we mean by 'story' includes the means by which the writer of imaginative literature projects his vision of reality, then we have arrived in critical theory, finally, at an approach to a literary work as functional for Chaucer, for Fielding, for Defoe as it is for James Joyce, for William Faulkner, and for Virginia Woolf.

Chapter Five

THE RHETORIC OF
'TO THE LIGHTHOUSE'

F ROM her critical essays we know that Virginia
Woolf saw a work of fiction as something having many
facets, something we can never know perfectly or completely. And from her fiction we know that her sense of
reality originated in her belief that impressions—the
'shower of innumerable atoms'—which bombard the
nervous system from the inception of awareness to the end,
are really all that one can ever know. It was, perhaps more
than anything else, from this metaphysical bias that her
mature literary method evolved, a method which would
allow her to communicate the countless and varied
impressions of her imaginary people.

Everything registered by the mind was, for her, 'the
proper stuff of fiction, every feeling, every thought, every
quality of brain and spirit. . . .'[1] This deeply rooted belief
caused her, after her second novel, to discard the traditional form of fiction and to create a form suitable for
projecting her own unique vision. It was, moreover, from
her intense preoccupation with human beings and their
relationship to each other and to reality that she developed
fully, in her later work, the delicate art of exploring
human experience and human associations. Of primary
importance to her was the problem of rendering aesthetically with words what the process of living felt like, how
her fictional people experienced life.

In her essay, 'Modern Fiction', Virginia Woolf made
clear her discontent with the form of the novel as represented by Wells, Galsworthy, and Bennett:

Admitting the vagueness which afflicts all criticism of

novels, let us hazard the opinion that for us at this moment the form of fiction most in vogue more often misses than secures the thing we seek. Whether we call it life or spirit, truth or reality, this, the essential thing, has moved off, or on, and refuses to be contained any longer in such ill-fitting vestments as we provide. Nevertheless, we go on persever-ingly, conscientiously, constructing our two and thirty chapters after a design which more and more ceases to resemble the vision in our minds.[2]

The conventional form, for Mrs Woolf, seemed not only to diminish but even to distort her vision of experience, of life, which, when artistically ordered, was to appear

> a luminous halo, a semi-transparent envelope surrounding us from the beginning of consciousness to the end.

She says further:

> Let us record the atoms as they fall upon the mind in the order in which they fall, let us trace the pattern, however disconnected and incoherent in appearance, which each sight or incident scores upon the consciousness.[3]

Through labour and perseverance, she arrived at a method, finally, which enabled her to realize her vision and to translate it into an aesthetically satisfying literary design.

To the Lighthouse, generally considered her finest novel, bears eloquent testimony to her mastery of a complex and disciplined form. In it she was able to present, within severely circumscribed limits of time, a wide range and multiplicity of experience by subtle and constant move-ments in and out of the minds of her various *personae*. With lucidity and sureness, she selected out of the flux and chaos of appearances certain thoughts, feelings, and impressions and arranged them in that skillful juxtaposition and sequence not only to produce a beautifully textured and formally composed whole, but also to render the fabric of experience which conformed to her own singular and sensitive vision.

The external structure of *To the Lighthouse* is not in the least complicated. It is composed of three parts of unequal length of which the first and longest section, 'The Window', covers the better part of a day; in it are introduced all the principal characters as well as the central issue: whether or not an expedition to the Lighthouse will take place on the morrow. The second and shortest section, 'Time Passes', is somewhat of a choral interlude and marks the passage of ten years; it also reveals, parenthetically, the death of several members of the family. The third movement, 'The Lighthouse', follows, which as in the first, covers less than a day, and in which the trip to the Lighthouse, suggested ten years earlier, is finally made.

This, then, is the simple outward structure of the novel and, in its broadest outline, the story it tells. But this bare summary is pure deception: 'story' in the conventional sense was not Virginia Woolf's interest. Perhaps Neville, in *The Waves*, is her spokesman when he says of Bernard:

> Let him burble on, telling us stories, while we lie recumbent. Let him describe what we have all seen so that it becomes a sequence. Bernard says there is always a story. I am a story. Louis is a story. There is the story of the boot-boy, the story of the man who sells winkles. Let him burble on with his story while I lie back and regard the stiff-legged figures of the padded batsmen through the trembling grasses.

Mrs Woolf was concerned with exploring the quality and complexity of human relationships; and to translate her explorations to the novel form, she had to abandon that series of dramatic events by which the conventional novel arrested and sustained interest and in its place to create moments of human consciousness. She had further to juxtapose those moments in such a way so as to effect a sequence, the arrangement of which would enlarge and enrich the moments already traversed as well as those to be encountered—in brief, to create an order in which the multiple contents of consciousness would, at any particular moment, illuminate the past and anticipate the future. Thus it was not for her to 'describe *what* we have all seen so that it becomes a sequence', but rather more to describe *how* her people have experienced what they have seen, and *how* all of these experiences stand in relation to one another and to some central principle. It is out of this concern that she achieved a unity of design that crowns her triumph in *To the Lighthouse*.

In an essay on Virginia Woolf, William Troy wrote that ' "Method" in fiction narrows down to nothing more or less than the selection of a point of view from which character may be studied and presented.'[4] As a possible critical approach, this statement may be perfectly valid. But its surface simplicity vanishes immediately we consider that Mrs Woolf did not confine herself to *a* single point of view: she used many to fashion her novel; and the problem of studying these points of view is compounded, moreover, by the fact that the characters, through whose minds the material is being filtered, are not established for us at the beginning of the book; they are given to us piecemeal, elusively; so that even at the end, though we see them in their entirety, we do not necessarily see them conclusively. The fact is that, more often than not, when we have finished one of her novels, although our imaginative sympathy has been aroused and enlarged, our knowledge of the character remains incomplete; he remains the sum of our impressions, a fluid personality.

The method, then, of creating these fictional people is, in a sense, additive: our own impression grows as the character's reflections and impressions—as well as those he elicits from others—grow. Thus our understanding too, in a sense, is additive: it is a continual synthesis of accumulated impressions. It would be more accurate, then, to modify Troy's statement and say that Mrs Woolf *creates* a point of view; she does not 'select' one. And we, as readers, are invited to recreate, through the process of reflexive reading, a portrait of the character in much the same creative manner.

The method can best be demonstrated if we look first at Mrs Ramsay, who, among principal narrators, is one of the most important, and observe the manner in which she is presented to us. I will confine myself *only* to the material transmitted to us through her consciousness—and in the *order* in which it is transmitted.

By restricting ourselves to Mrs Ramsay's point of view, solely to her reflections on and impressions of events and people, untempered by the thoughts and impressions she elicits from those around her, we are essentially deducing her personality and character as might spectators trapped in a single consciousness; and it is from this kind of separation and isolation—artificial as it necessarily is—that we begin to glean the progression of her mental activity, in all its depth and variety, which communicates the iridescence of her innermost self, that 'semi-transparent envelope' surrounding her as a human personality.

The opening statement of the novel belongs to Mrs Ramsay as she speaks to her son. Our next glimpse of her comes through the visual impression she receives of him. When her husband contradicts her forecast for the next day, he appears, in her mind, to be 'grinning sarcastically . . . disillusioning his son and casting ridicule' upon her (10). She senses his pride in the accuracy of his judgment but knows that

> What he said was true. It was always true. He was incapable of untruth; never tampered with a fact; never altered a disagreeable word to suit the pleasure or convenience of any mortal being, least of all his own children . . . (10–11).

With great economy, Mrs Woolf has given us in less than three pages a small but vivid picture of Mrs Ramsay's relationship to her son and to her husband as well as a dab or two of the colours contained on her emotional palette; and a little further we are given some idea of her generosity for the Lighthouse keeper, her sympathy for his isolation, and, in general, her desire to comfort those less fortunate creatures needing her bounty.

Throughout these opening pages we are easily persuaded over to Mrs Ramsay's side because she represents the maternity, the sympathy, and the charity that we place high in our scale of values. And we tend to feel averse to Mr Ramsay (and to Tansley) for having contradicted and upset the person who has engaged our sympathy. If Tansley, for example, is odious to her for having disappointed her son, then he is also odious to us.

Our intimacy increases when we see, a little further on, a few details of her physical appearance and share with her some private feelings:

> When she looked in the glass and saw her hair grey, her cheek sunk, at fifty, she thought possibly she might have managed things better—her husband; money; his books. But for her own part she would never for a single second regret her decision, evade difficulties, or slur over duties (14).

The tinge of self-pity in these lines is overshadowed by our admiration for this paradigm of selflessness.

Her trip to town with Tansley is both interesting and revealing. Before departing with this young man she had earlier thought odious, she stops to ask Carmichael if there is anything she can get him. But there is nothing he wants. And as if prompted by her sense of uselessness to Carmichael, she confides his past to Tansley, telling him of the early and unsuccessful marriage, the poverty, the hardship, the gradual decay—possibly aware that this confidence will flatter Tansley, make him feel important. But in the midst of this, she sees a circus bill and, forgetting momentarily her pity for Carmichael, suggests that they all go. Having given her companion, by that suggestion, an opportunity to bewail his own history of poverty and hardship, she reflects that she

> saw now why going to the circus had knocked him off his perch, poor little man, and why he came out, instantly, with all that about his father and mother and brothers and sisters. ... What he would have liked, she supposed, would have been to say that he had gone not to the circus but to Ibsen with the Ramsays. He was an awful prig—oh yes, an insufferable bore (22).

Indeed, even out of context, this passage indicates none of the kindness and charity we have been led to expect from Mrs Ramsay. In fact her thoughts reflect a tone of condescension and antipathy.

Here Virginia Woolf begins to enlarge the image of Mrs Ramsay by applying some sharply identifying strokes to her portrait. When, for example, her husband rebukes her for questioning his judgment about the weather, she ponders his callousness:

> To pursue truth with such astonishing lack of consideration for other people's feelings, to rend the thin veils of civilization so wantonly, so brutally, was to her so horrible an outrage of human decency that, without replying, dazed and blinded, she bent her head as if to let the pelt of jagged hail, the drench of dirty water, bespatter her unrebuked. ...
> She was quite ready to take his word for it, she said. Only then they need not cut sandwiches—that was all. They came to her, naturally, since she was a woman, all day long with this and that; one wanting this; another that; the children were growing up; she often felt she was nothing but a sponge sopped full of human emotions. Then he said, Damn you. He said, It must rain. He said, It won't rain; and instantly a Heaven of security opened before her. There was nobody she reverenced more. She was not good enough to tie his shoe strings, she felt (51).

Her reaction to his heedlessness of others' feelings is valid enough; and so perhaps is the idea that she is a sponge saturated with human emotions. What is curious, however, is the end of her reflection: her feeling 'not good enough to tie his shoe strings', because the thought which follows, although interspersed with other elements, begins a steady progression towards a very contradictory tendency in her personality. Knowing that her husband is ashamed for his outburst, she imagines him wanting to be 'warmed and soothed, to have his senses restored to him, his barrenness made fertile. . .' (59), and a disagreeable sensation comes over her, a sudden physical fatigue the genesis of which is too distasteful to put into words: and it is precisely her feeling of superiority over Mr Ramsay:

> . . . she did not like, even for a second, to feel finer than her husband; and further, could not bear not being entirely sure, when she spoke to him, of the truth of what she said. Universities and people wanting him, lectures and books and their being of the highest importance—all that she did not doubt for a moment; but it was their relation, and his coming to her like that, openly, so that any one could see, that discomposed her; for then people said he depended on her, when they must know that of the two he was infinitely the more important, and what she gave the world, in comparison with what he gave, negligible (61–62).

How significant it is that Mrs Ramsay, for all her self-sacrificing and goodness, even her tendency towards self-depreciation, should suddenly dwell on her husband's inferiority to her! should shortly be reminded of his financial inadequacy, to suspect that his last book 'was not quite his best'. These thoughts possibly reinforce her deepest, *unrecognized* feelings of his failure and her success. And just how disturbing that idea is to her, we shall see when this fundamental rift in her personality begins to reveal more significant ramifications.

It is important here only to notice that in this state of mind, she sees Carmichael shuffle by and is painfully 'reminded of the inadequacy of human relationships . . .' (62). Her cerebral excursion here is no less significant than the earlier one. Carmichael, we recall, wants nothing from her, needs nothing of her; and she feels uncomfortable because she interprets it as his not trusting her. So again her thoughts turn to the ugliness of *his* life: his opium addiction, his miserable wife, his poverty, his slovenliness. How much she went out of her way to make him like her (here a fleeting sense of her own beauty flashes through her mind):

> And after all . . . she had not generally any difficulty in making people like her. . . . Tears had flown in her presence. Men, and women too, letting go the multiplicity of things, had allowed themselves with her the relief of simplicity. It injured her that he [Carmichael] should shrink. It hurt her. And yet not cleanly, not rightly (64–65).

Indeed not rightly. Carmichael's frustrating her desire to give forces her to turn inwards, to plumb some dark recess, to suspect her own motives:

> . . . all this desire of hers to give, to help, was vanity. For her own self-satisfaction was it that she wished so instinctively to help, to give, that people might say of her, 'O Mrs Ramsay! dear Mrs Ramsay . . . Mrs Ramsay, of course!' and need her and send for her and admire her? Was it not secretly this that she wanted, and therefore when Mr Carmichael shrank away from her, as he did this moment, making off to some corner where he did acrostics endlessly, she did not feel merely snubbed back in her instinct, but made aware of the pettiness of some part of her, and of human relations, how flawed they are, how despicable, how self-seeking at their best (65–66).

Notice particularly how, though certainly not aware of it, she moves the burden of responsibility away from herself as a particular individual to 'human relations' in general: 'how flawed *they* are . . . how self-seeking at *their* best'.

It is understandable, in light of her utterance, why she finds Carmichael disquieting or why 'she did in her own heart infinitely prefer boobies to clever men' (85) or even why 'she would have liked to keep for ever [her two youngest children] just as they were, demons of wickedness, angels of delight, never to see them grow up into long-legged monsters' (89): boobies and children can be manœuvered, controlled, can be made to worship her.

Possibly there is something to one woman's charge that Mrs Ramsay was

'robbing her of her daughter's affections' . . . . Wishing to dominate, wishing to interfere, making people do what she wished . . . and she [Mrs Ramsay] thought it most unjust: How could she help being 'like that' to look at? No one could accuse her of taking pains to impress. She was often ashamed of her own shabbiness. Nor was she domineering, nor was she tyrannical. It was more true about hospitals and drains and the dairy (88–89).

Here again several significant observations can be made. In the first place, the charge brought against her makes no mention of the way she looked; yet in her self-defence, her appearance takes priority; and the sartorial deficit, as it were, becomes, in her mind, suddenly transformed into a kind of spiritual asset. Her shabbiness, we might suspect, is part of the trapping that belongs to her self-depreciating apparatus with which she plays out the larger drama of gaining sympathy, first; and getting people to do what she wished, second. Also notice here the way in which she absolves herself of any charge whatever by turning her attention to her community endeavours—the hospital, the drains, the dairy—the larger causes which quite naturally cancel out any accusation, however valid, levelled at her.

Despite these and many other defensive measures to which Mrs Ramsay is unconsciously given, she is not without her moments of awareness, moments when she is by herself and can be herself, when she need not think of others:

To be silent; to be alone. All the being and the doing, expansive, glittering, vocal, evaporated; and one shrunk, with a sense of solemnity, to being oneself, a wedge-shaped core

of darkness, something invisible to others. . . . When life
sank down for a moment . . . the range of experience
seemed limitless. And to everybody there was this sense of
unlimited resources, she supposed; one after another, she,
Lily, Augustus Carmichael, must feel, our apparitions, the
things you know us by, are simply childish. Beneath it is all
dark, it is all spreading, it is unfathomably deep; but now
and again we rise to the surface and that is what you see
us by (95–96).

As one who practises the art of creating human relationships, it is not surprising that she singles out Lily Briscoe
and Carmichael as those who share her sensibility; all three
are involved in creating aesthetic harmony out of human
experience: Carmichael with words, Lily with pigments,
Mrs Ramsay with people.

But Mrs Ramsay, for all her catalytic function in
bringing people together, is herself an extremely isolated
person. She is unable to share her deepest feelings with
anyone, unable to open herself spontaneously to express
freely her anger or her hurt or her love. Unlike her
husband, she must conceal her moods. Her relationship
to Mr Ramsay is, in fact, a fairly accurate index of the
aloofness and estrangement which lurk at the very core
of her 'wedge of darkness'. The walk she and Mr Ramsay
take before dinner is evidence enough. She speaks of
the many commonplace things that have probably been
spoken of before. And the tone becomes increasingly
strained, because her mind is wandering: the dahlias; the
fifty pounds it would cost to fix the greenhouse; whether
flower bulbs should be sent down; all the poverty and
suffering in the world; would her husband apologize for
saying 'Damn you'; his inability to see the simple things
around him; his tiresome phrase-making and melancholy;
his awkward habit of talking aloud. Then her mind turns
to his intellectual prowess and, while examining a fresh
mole hill on the bank, reflects that

. . . a great mind like his must be different in every way

from ours. All the great men she had ever known, she thought, deciding that a rabbit must have got in, were like that, and it was good for young men (though the atmosphere of the lecture-rooms was stuffy and depressing to her beyond endurance almost) simply to hear him. But without shooting rabbits, how was one to keep them down? she wondered (108).

Here is Virginia Woolf in one of her most brilliant moments, rendering dramatically the remoteness and isolation of a woman who does not, will not, *can not* share her husband's world. But more important than that, she unwittingly demeans him by the unflattering juxtaposition of her thoughts: rabbits ruining her flowers set on the same level of importance as her husband's academic stature! It is little wonder that Mrs Ramsay finds human relationships inadequate.

If this is the extent of the spiritual kinship she shares with her husband, we have legitimate cause to question her relationship to the others surrounding her; to question her sensitivity to the things in their lives they value most. How aware is she of Carmichael other than of the fact that she feeds and pities him? What is her interest in Lily other than her desire to see her married to Bankes? And Tansley? To what extent is she able or willing to understand the drives that make him so obnoxiously assertive? Are all her alliances undergirded by some self-seeking tendency? Does her need for match-making originate in the satisfaction of feeling her mastery over others? Or does she feel somehow ill-suited to her own match?

If we examine the memorable scene of the dinner party, we discover that Virginia Woolf has added several remarkable strokes to her constantly growing portrait. 'But what have I done with my life?' asks Mrs Ramsay taking her place at the head of the table, as a painter might before his canvas or a poet before his blank sheet. For she is surrounded by a group of antagonistic personalities, each concealing his resentment by mouthing empty shibboleths or by keeping silence. This is the assembly, and these are her materials. Out of them she must create something harmonious and whole, each part articulating smoothly with the next. And she is weary to the task: 'the whole of the effort of merging and flowing and creating rested on her' (126). She looks at her husband 'all in a heap, frowning' and wonders how she had ever felt any emotion or affection for him; she looks critically at Tansley and notes that he was 'thinking of himself and the impression he was making'; she looks at Bankes and thinks '—poor man! who had no wife, and no children and dined alone in lodgings . . .'; and she looks at Carmichael with that characteristic mixture of fraternal commiseration and maternal protectiveness.

While she surveys these people in their most pitiable, least commendable aspect, she begins to draw them together: a comment here; a question there; a spark of interest to urge Tansley on; an appeal to Lily; a piece of beef for Bankes. And when she has brought together this 'house full of unrelated passions', as she feels, under her aegis, she leaves them to themselves and drifts off to her own private world where she can stand aloof and look at the success of her clever and controlling handiwork:

Now she need not listen. It could not last, she knew, but at the moment her eyes were so clear that they seemed to go round the table unveiling each of these people, and their thoughts and their feelings, without effort like a light stealing under water so that its ripples and the reeds in it and the minnows balancing themselves, and the sudden silent trout are all lit up hanging, trembling. So she saw them; she heard them; but whatever they said had also this quality, as if what they said had the movement of a trout when, at the same time, one could see the ripple and the gravel, something to the right, something to the left; and the whole is held together; for whereas in active life she would be netting and separating one thing from another; she would be saying she liked the Waverley novels or had not read them; she would be urging herself forward; now she said nothing (160–61).

But though she is saying nothing, it is clear from the liveliness of her thoughts and images that her weariness has disappeared: the energizing centre in her being has become operative, as she moves these people about, according to her design.

The evolution of Paul's and Minta's engagement and Mrs Ramsay's part in it provide us with more evidence indicative of her personality. We know already that she has worked to make the connection between them; and when they arrive late for the dinner gathering, all aglow, Mrs Ramsay knows that

> It must have happened . . . they were engaged. And for a moment she felt what she had never expected to feel— jealousy. For he, her husband, felt it too—Minta's glow; he liked these girls, these golden-reddish girls, with something flying, something a little wild and harum-scarum about them. . . . There was some quality which she herself had not, some lustre, some richness, which attracted him, amused him, led him to make favourites of girls like Minta. . . . But indeed she was not jealous, only, now and then, when she made herself look in her glass a little resentful that she had grown old, perhaps, by her own fault (149).

Her jealousy of Minta and resentment at her years are somewhat perplexing: not so much that she has these feelings, for they are natural enough; but that she feel them at this particular time, when she should be happy for the pair whose union she has brought about. It seems contradictory that a woman so dedicated to the welfare and happiness of others dwell at such length on herself and her own imaginary losses. And as her thoughts return again to Minta and Paul ('. . . for her part she liked her boobies. Paul must sit by her. She had kept a place for him') and her dinner that will celebrate the occasion, she thinks profoundly of a man's love for a woman and then

74

thinks almost jeeringly of 'these lovers, these people entering into illusion glittering eyed, [who] must be danced round with mockery . . .' (151). Here are words inspired by feelings poignant in their disillusionment and bitterness.

Shortly after the assembly has dispersed, however, Mrs Ramsay, alone up stairs, attempts to stabilize herself from the disruptive feelings battling within her; she tries to smother that deeply buried conflict which caused the jealousy and resentment to spring forth at the thought of the engagement. Unaware of the real source of these feelings, she attempts to effect a moment of artificial stability, as it were, and thinks: 'Yes, that was done then, accomplished; and as with all things done, became solemn.' But we gain another insight into Mrs Ramsay when we realize that the solemnity of the event is, for her, buttressed on every side by her participation in it and their grateful memory of it:

They would . . . however long they lived, come back to this night; this moon; this wind; this house: and to her too. It flattered her, where she was most susceptible to flattery, to think how wound about in their hearts, however long they lived she would be woven . . . (170).

How necessary it is for her always to be at the centre of things, to have a kind of spiritual immortality live on in them after she is gone, to put them in her debt.

What is so conspicuous here, as in her relations with others, is her concern not so much with Paul or Minta, or with anyone else, as with herself: with the effect she has in directing the lives of others, while simultaneously claiming their approval and admiration and praise—that endless affirmation upon which her own temporary sense of self-assurance depends. She is indeed a woman who knows little contentment or security.

In the final scene with her husband, we are given the last significant details of Mrs Ramsay's portrait. Her reaction to his prediction of the next day's weather, at

the beginning of the section, recall, was one of unex-
pressed anger. And throughout the section, reading
sequentially only her thoughts and impressions, I have
been trying to suggest that her anger remained mute,
because she felt herself, above all, an appeasing, a concil-
iatory person, one who placed others first, who felt herself
subordinate to her husband—his work, his fame. Yet in
this closing scene, that contradictory part of her, that has
throughout suggested itself repeatedly, wells to the surface
for the last and most memorable time. Mr Ramsay, she
imagines, is looking at her and wants her to say that she
loves him, something she can not—will not—do:

> . . . she never told him that she loved him, but it was not
> so—it was not so. It was only that she never could say what
> she felt.

She fancies that he is looking at her, thinking,

> You are more beautiful than ever. And she felt herself very
> beautiful. Will you not tell me just once that you love me
> (185)?

But for all her compliance and sympathy and unselfish-
ness, she will not yield: she says nothing. She merely smiles
and maintains her aloofness in even so small and so natural
a wish; and as though by this denial she has unwittingly
subordinated him, has repaid him for the hurt he had
earlier inflicted, has made him feel the force of her victory,
she says, ' "Yes, you were right. It's going to be wet tomorrow. You won't be able to go." ' And characteristic of her
propensity to overrate the imagination of others and to
fail to recognize her own motives, she believes that she has

> triumphed again. She had not said it: yet he knew.

Indeed, the ultimate triumph is hers: whether, as she
believes, in not expressing verbally her love; or, as she is
unable to realize, by frustrating her husband in an act of
retaliatory silence.

Our first introduction to Mr Ramsay is not a sympathetic one. His relentlessness in the matter of the trip to the Lighthouse, indeed, strikes a negative chord. His intellectualism is harsh and uncompromising; his logic will not be tampered with; his opinions will not be questioned. When his wife asks him, for example, how he can be so sure about the weather, his reaction is not only violent but also revealing:

> The extraordinary irrationality of her remark, the folly of women's minds enraged him. He had ridden through the valley of death, been shattered and shivered; and now, she flew in the face of facts, made his children hope what was utterly out of the question, in effect, told lies. He stamped his foot on the stone step. 'Damn you,' he said (50).

That her remark should seem extraordinarily irrational to a mind so disciplined is not unusual; nor is it unusual that his philosophical orientation should cause him to interpret such uncertain promises as lies. What is interesting, however, is his fantasy: his seeing himself struggling heroically in the Light Brigade in the valley of death at Balaclava. Part of his rage is undoubtedly from the sudden injury done to the splendid self-image he is momentarily experiencing. While such outbursts are not especially encouraging to human relations, we might begin to ponder why, in reality, a man of his intellectual stature should, in fantasy, entertain such dreams of heroic grandeur.

A little further we are given a glimpse of his metaphysic; and we feel the barrenness and disunity of an epistemological vision which sees knowledge as an alphabet that one must plod through perseveringly, letter by letter, before reaching Z, before laying claim to genius. We learn also from this mental excursion his estimation of himself:

> In that flash of darkness he heard people saying—he was a failure—that R was beyond him. He would never reach R.

. . . He had not genius; he laid no claim to that: but he had, or might have had, the power to repeat every letter of the alphabet from A to Z accurately in order. . . . Yet he would not die lying down; he would find some crag of rock, and there, his eyes fixed on the storm, trying to the end to pierce the darkness, he would die standing. He would never reach R (54–55).

In light of this inside view, for all his harshness and severity, his seeming disregard for people, his outward sterility, we know that in his own company he is ruthlessly honest with himself; that his grandiose fantasies are compensatory measures to ward off the onslaught of feelings of inadequacy he experiences; further, that the sympathy and assurance he craves are, for him, urgent and human needs—the very needs which the others find degrading.

Indeed

Who shall blame him, if, so standing for a moment, he dwells upon fame, upon search parties, upon cairns raised by grateful followers over his bones? . . . Who will not secretly rejoice when the hero puts his armour off, and halts by the window and gazes at his wife and son, who very distant at first, gradually come closer and closer, till lips and book and head are clearly before him, though still lovely and unfamiliar from the intensity of his isolation and the waste of ages and the perishing of the stars, and finally putting his pipe in his pocket and bending his magnificent head before her—who will blame him if he does homage to the beauty of the world (57)?

The atmosphere of his mind is lonely and brooding; but facing squarely the dark of human ignorance in a world of misery, he knows that

he was for the most part happy; he had his wife; he had his children; he had promised in six weeks' time to talk 'some nonsense' to the young men of Cardiff . . . (70).

Neither we, as readers, nor those surrounding him acknowledge the sensitivity his utterances bear out. While meditating on the terrace, for example, he passes Mrs Ramsay and notes the

> sternness at the heart of her beauty. It saddened him, and her remoteness pained him, and he felt, as he passed, that he could not protect her, and, when he reached the hedge, he was sad. He could do nothing to help her. He must stand by and watch her. Indeed, the infernal truth was, he made things worse for her (98–99).

In the course of the novel Mr Ramsay repeatedly owns up to most of his many shortcomings; and in his sincerest reflections, we find little of the self-depreciation that permeates his wife's musing. Here rather we have self-evaluation, for good or ill, that is forthright, without self-pity, at times, almost boyish in its naïveté. Despite the charges constantly brought against him for his sympathy-mongering, we might begin, legitimately to suspect that much of it is the result of Mrs Ramsay's distance, her solitude—that estrangement which inevitably exacts from him, too, the price of being alone. He knows that she will not permit him entry into her world; he knows as well that she can not share his. Their walk through the garden, discussed earlier, supports eloquently the testament of her, and consequently his, enforced isolation. But even under these circumstances, he is not only acquiescent, but loyal and even grateful:

> The father of eight children—he reminded himself. And he would have been a beast and a cur to wish a single thing altered. Andrew would be a better man than he had been. Prue would be a beauty, her mother said. They would stem the flood a bit. That was a good bit of work on the whole—his eight children. They showed he did not damn the poor little universe entirely . . . (106).

If we divest Mr Ramsay of all the judgments crowded on his image by the other *personae* and attend only to those reflections and impressions which originate in him, we find a very different image emerging. His intellectual life may seem austere, uncompromising, rigorously dedicated to fact; but as a husband and father, he is indeed not only more devoted than his wife to those who make up his world, but also more honest than she in his dealings with them. As egotistical or tryannical or cruel or barren as the others may choose to see him, his effectiveness as a man becomes apparent when he acknowledges James' steering. He has only to say two words: 'Well done!' to transform his son's world, to establish finally the union between father and son. And with all this we might ponder the validity of his being the 'arid scimitar'; we might even begin to question the reliability of those *personae* who throughout the novel heap negative judgments on the man.

The problem of deducing James Ramsay offers no special difficulty since emotionally he remains fairly constant throughout. We know from the first page that the boy has been promised a trip to the Lighthouse, and his mother's reassuring words to that effect convey to him 'an extraordinary joy'. But his reaction to his father's contention that the weather will not permit the expedition is startlingly forceful:

> Had there been an axe handy, or a poker, any weapon that would have gashed a hole in his father's breast and killed him, there and then, James would have seized it (10).

It seems reasonable to assume from James' thought that his mother 'was ten thousand times better in every way than he [Mr Ramsay] was', that the violence in his first response was not just of the moment but rather a violence which has always characterized his relation to his father.

A little further on his jealousy towards the Lighthouse keeper's son, for whom Mrs Ramsay is knitting stockings, indicates the possessiveness he feels for his mother as well as his unwillingness to share with anyone the attentions

which, he feels, should be exclusively his own. His jealousy
is again stimulated when his father interrupts the story
Mrs Ramsay is reading to him:

> . . . He hated the twang and twitter of his father's emotions
> which, vibrating round them, disturbed the perfect sim-
> plicity and good sense of his relations with his mother. By
> looking fixedly at the page, he hoped to make him move on;
> by pointing his finger at the word, he hoped to recall his
> mother's attention, which, he knew angrily, wavered in-
> stantly his father stopped (58).

In a short image-freighted passage, Mrs Woolf helps us to
discern, in metaphoric terms, his feelings for each parent

> as he stood stiff between her knees, felt her rise in a rosy-
> flowered fruit tree laid with leaves and dancing boughs into
> which the beak of brass, the arid scimitar of his father, the
> egotistical man, plunged and smote, demanding sympathy
> (60).

These are the impressions of a six-year-old boy. Ten years
later when he is in the boat with his father and his sister,
Cam, we discover no appreciable difference in his relation
to Mr Ramsay: the rivalry and jealousy are still vivid. His
rage is immediately mobilized when he thinks he will lose
Cam to him; and he stares hatefully at his father, seeing
him again as

> that fierce sudden black-winged harpy, with its talons and
> its beak all cold and hard, that struck and struck at you
> . . . (273).

He searches his memory for the cause of his hatred and
terror, trying to find some image which will concretize his
feeling, and envisions himself as the helpless child watching
a wagon crush someone's foot. As he twists backward
through the labyrinth of his mind, he recalls the world of
his childhood where the feeling he now harbours was
first nourished:

> It was in this world that the wheel went over the person's

foot. Something, he remembered, stayed and darkened over him; would not move; something flourished up in the air, something arid and sharp descended even there, like a blade, a scimitar, smiting through the leaves and flowers even of that happy world and making it shrivel and fall (275).

He recalls the first time he felt the urge to kill his father, the time his helplessness was terrifying, when his mother

had gone stiff all over, and then, her arm slackening, so that he felt she listened to him no longer, she had risen somehow and gone away and left him there, impotent, ridiculous, sitting on the floor grasping a pair of scissors (277–278).

If we consider James in terms of his possessiveness for his mother, his rivalry and jealousy for his father, his insatiable need for paternal recognition, his sense of impotence and rage, and the pervasive anxiety which conditions his introspection, we might easily attach to him a Freudian label and summarily dismiss him as a victim modelled after that prototype of antiquity. But to do so, to resort to that kind of verbal shorthand, would be to ignore the richness and sensitivity to detail with which he was created. We would miss, in addition, the artistry with which Virginia Woolf, in three short sentences, beautifully crystallizes the response of an adolescent who has just found a father:

He was so pleased that he was not going to let anybody share a grain of his pleasure. His father had praised him. They must think that he was perfectly indifferent (306).

Outside the Ramsay family there are several other centres of consciousness whose tenuous insights and impressions add to the complex integration of the work. William Bankes is one of them. Because he never emerges forcefully, readers often fail to see him as the extremely deceptive character he is; and the success of Virginia Woolf's cumulative method of characterization, to a large extent, keeps the deception inconspicuous. Only when we isolate and study his point of view in its particular sequence, do we begin to organize a more accurate picture of his personality and character. If the reader said, for instance, that William Bankes was a selfish man who gave precedence to his work because he was unable to establish meaningful human ties, the statement would probably be met with zealous disapprobation. If he said, that he disapproved of in Mr Ramsay the very things he himself was guilty of and, moreover, was jealous of Ramsay for having what he himself would have liked; if he said, that like Peer Gynt, his motto in life was: 'To thine own self be enough'; that human beings were really an interference with one's own ambitions, the author of those statements would likely be charged with that critical irresponsibility which marks all rash interpretations. Yet these suggestions are worth exploring.

Our first introduction to William Bankes occurs when he is observing Lily Briscoe:

> Her shoes were excellent, he observed. They allowed the toes their natural expansion. Lodging in the same house with her, he had noticed too, how orderly she was, up before breakfast and off to paint, he believed, alone: poor, presumably, and without the complexion or the allurement of Miss Doyle certainly, but with a good sense which made her in his eyes superior to that young lady (31).

The observation is cool, critical, detached. He sees her more an intelligent and systematic schedule than a woman.

Further on he ruminates on his friendship with Mr Ramsay and how its 'pulp had gone', how 'repetition had taken the place of newness'. Yet

> He was anxious for the sake of this friendship and perhaps too in order to clear himself in his own mind from the imputation of having dried and shrunk. . . . He was anxious that Lily Briscoe should not disparage Ramsay (a great man

in his own way) yet should understand how things stood between them (35).

The curious thought that Lily might disparage Ramsay is clarified when we sense the subtle disparagement Bankes himself indulges in against his old friend:

> ... He weighed Ramsay's case, commiserated him, envied him, as if he had seen him divest himself of all the glories of isolation and austerity which crowned him in youth to cumber himself definitely with fluttering wings and clucking domesticities. . . . Could one help noticing that habits grew on him? eccentricities, weaknesses perhaps? It was astonishing that a man of his intellect could stoop so low as he did —but that was too harsh a phrase—could depend so much as he did upon people's praise (37–38).

Even in evaluating Mr Ramsay's work, what appears on the surface as praise is, underneath, a smoldering criticism: an insinuation that Ramsay's academic life is finished:

> Times without number, he had said, 'Ramsay is one of those men who do their best work before they are forty.' He had made a definite contribution to philosophy in one little book when he was only five and twenty; what came after was more or less amplification, repetition (39).

When Lily admits her dislike for Mr Ramsay's narrowness, Bankes is quick to suggest to her that perhaps he was

> 'A bit of a hypocrite?' . . . for was he not thinking of his friendship, and of Cam refusing to give him a flower, and of all those boys and girls, and his own [Bankes'] house, full of comfort, but, since his wife's death, quiet rather? Of course, he had his work. . . . All the same, he rather wished Lily to agree that Ramsay was, as he said, 'a bit of a hypocrite' (72).

A strange wish indeed coming from someone who only minutes before was anxious that Lily should not disparage Ramsay!

At the dinner in which Mrs Ramsay has taken such

pains to please Bankes, we find him bored and annoyed,
yet characteristically 'preserving a demeanour of exquisite
courtesy'. He feels his very presence there a sacrifice on
his part:

> How trifling it all is, how boring it all is, he thought, com-
> pared with the other thing—work. Here he sat drumming
> his fingers on the table-cloth when he might have been—he
> took a flashing bird's-eye view of his work. What a waste of
> time it all was to be sure! Yet now, at this moment her
> presence meant absolutely nothing to him: her beauty meant
> nothing to him; her sitting with the little boy at the window
> —nothing, nothing. He wished only to be alone and to take
> up that book. He felt uncomfortable; he felt treacherous,
> that he could sit by her side and feel nothing for her. The
> truth was that he did not enjoy family life. It was in this
> sort of state that one asked oneself, What does one live for?
> Why, one asked oneself, does one take all these pains for the
> human race to go on? Is it so very desirable? Are we attrac-
> tive as a species? Not so very, he thought, looking at those
> rather untidy boys. His favourite, Cam, was in bed, he sup-
> posed. Foolish questions, vain questions, questions one
> never asked if one was occupied. Is human life this? Is
> human life that? One never had time to think about it. . . .
> He was sitting beside Mrs Ramsay and he had nothing in
> the world to say to her. . . . He must make himself talk.
> Unless he were very careful, she would find out this treachery
> of his; that he did not care a straw for her, and that would
> not be at all pleasant, he thought (134–135).

What is most striking here is Bankes' utter selfishness.
The whole of his discontent originates in his feeling himself that superior being whose claim on the success—
indeed on the immortality—of his work is being jeopard-
ized by this distasteful, time-consuming assembly. If we
watch carefully the play of his thoughts, we see that from
his aversion to family life, he moves on to question the
worth of the human race. But that question is quickly
checked with the thought that when one was occupied

one had no time to think of such things. The check is indeed revealing, because if he were to pursue the question, he would inevitably come face to face with the void in his own life—a life in which everything and everyone have been subordinated to the interest of his work and his fame; a life, moreover, made chilly by the emotional distance he has had to maintain between himself and others in the interest of that pursuit.

Charles Tansley's first appearance, like Mr Ramsay's, strikes the reader negatively. 'There'll be no landing at the Lighthouse tomorrow,' he says, hammering home his mentor's prediction, while compounding the disappointment both Mrs Ramsay and James feel. The impression he makes is indeed an objectionable one. For one thing, our initial opinion of him is reinforced by the aspersions heaped upon him by Mrs Ramsay:

> He was such a miserable specimen, the children said, all humps and hollows. He couldn't play cricket; he poked; he shuffled. He was a sarcastic brute . . . (15).

Secondly, the commentary offered by the Omniscient Narrator is subtly persuasive. For example:

> 'it's due west,' said the atheist Tansley, holding his bony fingers so that the wind blew through them, for he was sharing Mr Ramsay's evening walk up and down, up and down the terrace (12).

Indeed, in the context of the work, there is little to redeem Tansley from the hostility he arouses in his companions and consequently in the reader. It is not redemption, however, that we are after, since Mrs Woolf has not actually condemned him. It is true that the acid with which he was etched is often undiluted, and the laughter he inspires is often punitive. But underneath, Tansley is very different in quality from those other unamiable and often comic characters in the gallery of literature. His awkwardness, for example, is not that of a Uriah Heep; his obsequiousness is different in kind from that of Jane Austen's Pastor Collins; his hostility does not have the destructiveness of a Michael Henchard; nor does his aggressiveness have the threatening quality of a Tartuffe. And the reason is that Virginia Woolf bids us not to judge and condemn him, but rather to understand him, to see the source of his confusion of values; and Tansley's walk to the village with Mrs Ramsay offers some striking evidence to help us in that understanding. For example, he is flattered by Mrs Ramsay's invitation. He feels proud to be in her company—even a little chivalrous. He feels important in her confiding Carmichael's story to him. Soon he is feeling all sorts of things,

> something in particular which excited him and disturbed him for reasons which he could not give. He would like her to see him, gowned and hooded, walking in a procession. A fellowship, a professorship, he felt capable of anything . . . (20).

But the matter of the circus comes up and, suspending for the moment his fantasy of academic triumph, he makes an appeal for his companion's sympathy: he is almost overcome by the need to tell Mrs Ramsay that he had never been to a circus because

> It was a large family, nine brothers and sisters, and his father was a working man. 'My father is a chemist, Mrs Ramsay. He keeps a shop.' He himself had paid his own way since he was thirteen. Often he went without his greatcoat in winter. He could never 'return hospitality' (those were his parched stiff words) at college. He had to make things last twice the time other people did; he smoked the cheapest tobacco; shag; the same the old men did in the quays. He worked hard—seven hours a day . . . (21–22).

Preoccupied with his self-glorification, Tansley's arrogance and vindictiveness have a moment of calm, because alone with Mrs Ramsay, he is the centre of attention.

Only at the dinner party do we realize how urgent is his need to be that centre when we observe his anger at the light conversation; he is angry not so much because it is flimsy table talk, but rather more because it does not offer him the opportunity to flaunt his master mind, to vent his own defensive narcissism:

> . . . he was not going to talk the sort of rot these people wanted him to talk. He was not going to be condescended to by these silly women. He had been reading in his room, and now he came down and it all seemed to him silly, superficial, flimsy. . . . They did nothing but talk, talk, talk, eat, eat, eat. It was the women's fault. Women made civilization impossible with all their 'charm', all their silliness (129).

His anger reaches such intensity that he needs to externalize it somehow, to find some outside cause which will justify it and give him reason to feel exploited, to feel the pariah; and Lily Briscoe's request that Tansley take her to the Lighthouse comes at an opportune moment indeed: now she can assume the burden of the blame:

> She was telling lies he could see. She was laughing at him. He was in his old flannel trousers. He had no others. He felt very rough and isolated and lonely. He knew that she was trying to tease him for some reason; she didn't want to go to the Lighthouse with him; she despised him: so did Prue Ramsay; so did they all (130–131).

When we realize the extent of his sense of worthlessness, we can begin to appreciate why it is so necessary for him to project that feeling on to others, to feel it as coming from the outside. We also begin to appreciate his thought that 'if only he could be alone in his room . . . working among his books. That was where he was at his ease' (131). It is not difficult to understand his loneliness in terms of his disturbed relations with people; his feeling himself an object of pillory, the outcast of the Hebrides; his interpreting what others say as an attempt to humiliate him; his feeling such vigorous resentment for the company; and, consequently, his wishing to depreciate the Ramsays when the urge to assert himself is frustrated. Depreciating them would conversely appreciate him in his own mind. Thus the idea occurs to him that the Ramsays talked nonsense,

> and he pounced on this fresh instance with joy, making a note which, one of these days, he would read aloud, to one or two of his friends. There, in a society where one could say what one liked he would sarcastically describe 'staying with the Ramsays' and what nonsense they talked. It was worth while doing it once, he would say; but not again. The women bored one so, he would say. Of course Ramsay had dished himself by marrying a beautiful woman and having eight children (136).

And after having arrogantly vindicated the Ramsays, he returns to the smarting membrane of his tender vainglory and restores it with fantasies of his hidden grandeur and power and vengeance; because

> he was Charles Tansley—a fact that nobody there seemed to realize; but one of these days every single person would know it. . . .
> He could almost pity these mild cultivated people, who would be blown sky high, like bales of wool and barrels of apples, one of these days by the gunpowder that was in him (138).

Lily Briscoe, the artist, is, as David Daiches wrote, 'deputy for the author'.[5] It is in her effort to express her sense of reality through colour and form that we are exposed to some of the many aesthetic problems the artist faces in communicating his private vision to the world outside. But more than that, Lily Briscoe is of central importance in unifying the work. Hers is the principal consciousness through which Mrs Ramsay is kept vivid before the reader in the final movement of the novel. As deputy for the artist and as chief sentient centre, she is the reader's most reliable source of information and his most effective emotional and intellectual guide. More than any of the other *personae*, she expresses her ambivalence towards certain of the people, her inadequacy as human being and as artist, her sense of the strange admixture of emotional and intellectual and moral elements which undergirds human behaviour.

Our initial glimpse of Lily suggests immediately how well, for example, she understands Mr Ramsay. Standing by her easel, she hears him shouting ' "Boldly we rode and well",' and supposes that he is in one of those fantasies in which he imagines himself riding off 'to die gloriously . . . Upon the heights of Balaclava' (29). And she thinks,

> Never was anybody at once so ridiculous and so alarming. But so long as he kept like that, waving, shouting, she was safe; he would not stand still and look at her picture (29–30).

Later when Bankes suggests that Mr Ramsay was a 'bit of a hypocrite', however, we discover her sense of honesty and justice:

> Oh, no—the most sincere of men, the truest (here he was), the best; but, looking down, she thought, he is absorbed in himself, he is tyrannical, he is unjust (72).

But in spite of this, she knows that he has what Bankes has not:

> a fiery unworldliness; he knows nothing about trifles; he loves dogs and his children. He has eight. Mr Bankes has none. Did he not come down in two coats the other night and let Mrs Ramsay trim his hair into a pudding basin (40)?

She knows moreover the depth and strength of his feelings for his wife:

> For him to gaze as Lily saw him gazing at Mrs Ramsay was a rapture, equivalent, Lily felt, to the loves of dozens of young men. . . . It was love, she thought, pretending to move her canvas, distilled and filtered; love that never attempted to clutch its object; but, like the love which

mathematicians bear their symbols, or poets their phrases, was meant to be spread over the world and become part of the human gain (73–74).

Lily understands Mrs Ramsay too, her 'mania for marriage', her habit of 'presiding with immutable calm over destinies which she completely failed to understand' (78). Alert to Mrs Ramsay's seeing people as downtrodden and pitiable, she watches her looking at Bankes and thinks:

Why does she pity him? For that was the impression she gave, when she told him that his letters were in the hall. Poor William Bankes, she seemed to be saying, as if her own weariness had been partly pitying people, and the life in her, her resolve to live again, had been stirred by pity. And it was not true, Lily thought; it was one of those misjudgments of hers that seemed to be instinctive and to arise from some need of her own rather than of other people's (127–128).

This is only one example of Lily's perceptiveness; and how remarkably close she comes to the earlier appraisal of Mrs Ramsay. The image she conjures up of her sitting at the dinner is also a remarkable condensation of insight:

How childlike, how absurd she was, sitting up there with all her beauty opened again in her, talking about the skins of vegetables. There was something frightening about her. . . . Mrs Ramsay, Lily felt, as she talked about the skins of vegetables, exalted that, worshipped that; held her hands over it to warm them, to protect it, and yet, having brought it all about, somehow laughed, led her victims, Lily felt, to the altar (151–153).

Ten years later, a little embittered and more brittled by loneliness, Lily thinks back on Mrs Ramsay, now as someone who has

faded and gone. . . . We can over-ride her wishes, improve away her limited, old-fashioned ideas. She recedes further and further from us. Mockingly she seemed to see her there at the end of the corridor of years saying, of all incongruous things, 'Marry! Marry!' . . . And one would have to say to her, It has all gone against your wishes. They're happy like that; I'm happy like this. Life has changed completely. At that all her being, even her beauty, became for a moment, dusty and out of date. For a moment Lily . . . summing up the Rayleys, triumphed over Mrs Ramsay, who would never know how Paul went to coffee-houses and had a mistress; how he sat on the ground and Minta handed him his tools; how she stood here painting, had never married, not even William Bankes (260).

And having escaped Mrs Ramsay's domination and her compulsion to get people married, Lily felt that

now she could stand up to Mrs Ramsay—a tribute to the astonishing power that Mrs Ramsay had over one. Do this, she said, and one did it. Even her shadow at the window with James was full of authority (262).

One of the most significant aspects of Lily Briscoe's highly sophisticated sensibility, and one of her most sharply individualizing traits, is her ability to translate her own experience of human relations into subtle and profound insights. She is aware of the depth and diversity of impulses which govern human behaviour, impulses which cast human activity in endless enigmatic shadows, so that the sensitive observer wonders 'how many shapes a person might wear' (289). She is sensible to the imperfect vision one has of another; of the futility of attempting to know or to understand what goes on in another's 'wedge-shaped core of darkness'; of the inadequacy and obliquity of human relations. She looks at Carmichael and thinks how

they looked up at the sky and said it will be fine or it won't be fine. But this was one way of knowing people, she thought: to know the outline, not the detail, to sit in one's garden and look at the slopes of a hill running purple down into the distant heather (289).

She thinks back on Tansley and is reminded again of the selfish needs and pernicious self-interest which determine and shape one's notion of others:

> Her own idea of him was grotesque. . . . Half one's notions of other people were, after all, grotesque. They served private purposes of one's own. He did for her instead of a whipping boy. She found herself flagellating his lean flanks when she was out of temper. If she wanted to be serious about him she had to help herself to Mrs Ramsay's sayings, to look at him through her eyes (293).

She, too, questions the meaning of life. And clearly, poignantly, she articulates what she feels to be the cause of the ugliness and emptiness and shapelessness that hover over it: the inability to communicate with one another and create harmony out of the chaos of experience. Addressing herself silently to Carmichael, Lily knows that if she could put her question of life to him,

> if they both got up, here, now on the lawn, and demanded an explanation, why was it so short, why was it so inexplicable, said it with violence, as two fully equipped human beings from whom nothing should be hid might speak, then, beauty would roll itself up; *the space would fill;* those empty flourishes would form into shape (268).[6]

Significantly the Ramsay's landing at the Lighthouse signifies that sudden order in life that Lily seeks to express in art. Thus it is only when James has united with his father—their communication realized and their harmony established—that Lily sees finally and vividly, in the pattern of relationships on her canvas, the fleeting harmony that constitutes her vision. And indeed it is a vision which 'must be perpetually remade', just as human relations must be kept in a constant state of repair.

By isolating the various narrators and examining their sequential utterances, I have attempted to deduce and integrate the personality of each.[7] The method is necessary in analysing the multiple-point-of-view novel because it avoids impressionistic guesswork. Secondly, without examining extended passages it would be difficult for the reader to determine the *kind* of narrator he is dealing with; and without that knowledge, it would be almost impossible to evaluate either the reliability of that narrator's testimony or his impressions and biases.

In the most successful novels, the reader's judgment of a narrator is rigorously controlled (often without his being conscious of it) by rhetorical devices which I shall consider later; and there is generally no question in the reader's mind as to how he should feel about so and so or such and such at a particular time or in a particular context when the fictional material is presented by a particular narrator.

In a work as successfully wrought as *To the Lighthouse*, however, it is not uncommon to find evaluations made of the various *personae* which betray the critic's misunderstanding of them, and consequently a distortion in his interpretation of the work. For example, in the early pages of her analysis of the novel, Elizabeth Drew, in describing Mr and Mrs Ramsay, wrote:

> When her husband craves sympathy and reassurance, James feels her spirit rise 'in a rosy-flowered fruit tree laid with leaves and dancing boughs'. At the end of that scene, when as 'fountain and spray of life' she has refreshed 'the beak of brass, barren and bare' of her husband, [he departs] like a child who drops off satisfied. . . .[8]

The quotations Mrs Drew chose to describe husband and wife come from the section she is discussing (Chapter VII, 'The Window'). However, the opening sentence of that chapter is 'But his son hated him.' And following the brief section explaining, through James, the reason for the hatred, the angle of narration shifts to the Omniscient Narrator from whom we learn that

> into this delicious fecundity, this fountain and spray of life,

the fatal sterility of the male plunged itself, like a beak of
brass, barren and bare (58).

The validity of Mrs Drew's choice of quotation to
describe Mr and Mrs Ramsay would be unquestionable
were it not for the fact that it is an imagistic evaluation
which is carried over and developed further when we shift
back to James' point of view; when he

> felt all her strength flaring up to be drunk and quenched by
> the beak of brass, the arid scimitar of the male, which smote
> mercilessly, again and again, demanding sympathy (59).

The same image is further elaborated in the sixteen-year-
old James, who, in the boat with his father, remembers

> that fierce sudden black-winged harpy, with its talons and
> its beak all cold and hard, that struck and struck at you . . .
> (273).

who remembers also that

> something flourished up in the air, something arid and sharp
> descended even there, like a blade, a scimitar, smiting
> through the leaves and flowers even of that happy world
> and making it shrivel and fall (276).

It is noteworthy that with the older James, Mrs Woolf
does not call upon the Omniscient Narrator for any
commentary: the boy's vocabulary and image-forming
capacity are no longer limited as they were when he was
six years old. The images, now, and the words evoking
them are his own. We might legitimately conclude, then,
that although the Omniscient Narrator is utilized in the
earlier scene, his use was primarily to prepare us for, and
then, by reflexion, to support James' impression of his
father.

This scene is called to issue because it points out the way
in which a critic has attached the label of one biased
narrator,—one possibly most amenable to her own pre-
dilection—and then ignore Mr Ramsay's point of view
from which we discover his positive attributes. The

critical danger of failing to recognize the source of the information can, and often does, result in a serious obstacle to the understanding of the work as a whole. Mrs Drew's closing statements, that '. . . Mr Ramsay stands as a symbol of the sterile, destructive barriers to relationship,' that he is 'evoked in images of sterility, hardness and cruelty and of deliberate isolation',[9] are inaccurate especially when we recall James' landing at the Lighthouse and ponder those seeming 'sterile, destructive barriers to relationship'. To accept with finality Mrs Drew's evaluation of Mr Ramsay would be as serious a mis-evaluation of him as would our accepting Huckleberry Finn's appraisal of himself when he says that he is a very evil boy.

Other critics have failed to proceed with caution in the multiple-point-of-view novel. The picture of Mrs Ramsay, for example, that pervades most Woolfian criticism, is one of fertility and love and warmth and comfort and so on. To be sure, she is all of that. But to see only those qualities and to ignore her less flattering characteristics is to misread a vitally important part of the work. One of Virginia Woolf's often-quoted commentators, Bernard Blackstone, for instance, finds that the 'life lived in a perfect relationship is not possible between Mr and Mrs Ramsay because he is simply the demanding party, she simply the giving'.[10]

Mr Blackstone is simply a naïve and critically inept reader. For one thing, if Mr Blackstone were not so eager to resolve *who* is *what*, he would have realized that for Virginia Woolf that 'perfect relationship' is perfect sham. If we review the analyses given both these characters earlier, we will see that Mrs Ramsay, herself, questions her charity; ponders the charge of stealing affection; wonders if all her beneficence is rooted in some self-seeking. It is true that she gives a great deal; but her giving is not a *simple* matter, because unfortunately too many of her private needs depend, for their satisfaction, on her charity.

As for Mr Ramsay, it is true that he demands sympathy.

But whatever else he demands remains obscure, even with repeated readings of the text. The reason he may seem so demanding stems, in all probability, from our registering the impressions of the characters with whom we ally ourselves early in the novel; and as a consequence, we may tend to ignore many of Mr Ramsay's redeeming qualities, the most conspicuous of which are his devotion to his children and the unconditional love he bears his wife.

In another section, Mr Blackstone writes that 'Yet even for Charles Tansley Mrs Ramsay has affection, thinking of his struggles and his youth'.[11] But we need only review their walk to town during which Tansley tells her of his 'struggles and his youth', to discover her thinking:

He was an awful prig—oh yes, an insufferable bore. . . . But she would see to it that they (her children) didn't laugh at him any more (22).

In still another section, Mr Blackstone, writing of William Bankes, says he 'is a botanist, a widower . . . a bit of an old faddist, but *kindhearted* and *sincere*'.[12] We have only to reconstruct Mr Bankes' thoughts at the dinner party, to call the kindness of his heart to question; and as for his sincerity—it should not be necessary to mention again his wishing Lily Briscoe to agree with him that his friend, Mr Ramsay, was 'a bit of a hypocrite' (72).

These misjudgments of character are perhaps due to an occasional error in textual reading. In discussing the final scene between Lily and Mr Ramsay, for example, Mr Blackstone says that Lily 'does not seem to see what he wants from her. And suddenly, she looks down at his boots—'[13] and praises them. Again we turn to Part III of the novel, the first chapter of which is presented (with the exception of two short sentences) entirely through Lily's consciousness; and the second chapter which is shared between her and Mr Ramsay, to see that Lily *thinks* she knows very well why Mr Ramsay is bearing down on her: because he wants sympathy. And her praising his boots, instead, clarifies the issue in the following short paragraph:

'What beautiful boots!' she exclaimed. She was ashamed of herself. To praise his boots when he asked her to solace his soul; when he had shown her his bleeding hands, his lacerated heart, and asked her to pity them, then to say, cheerfully, 'Ah, but what beautiful boots you wear!' deserved, she knew, and she looked up expecting to get it, in one of his sudden roars of ill-temper, complete annihilation (229).

Mr Blackstone's failure to grasp the material of Lily Briscoe's point of view in one small section, may well be the very reason he finds in this novel—in which some twenty-three angles of perspective are modulated over three hundred pages—the final theme of 'love . . . married life, a family—' to be 'in the end this: a weary woman happy in her children, torn and exhausted by her husband, spreading the mantle of charity around her friends'.[14] As Mr Ramsay might say, 'Someone has blundered!'

If special attention is not paid to the points of view in a novel where they are creatively modulated, there is always the temptation to judge a character according to another character's judgment of him, especially when our judgment parallels that of a character who has engaged our sympathy.

Such is the case in James Hafley's commendable study, *The Glass Roof: Virginia Woolf as Novelist*.[15] In a section in which he discusses Ramsay, Mr Hafley agrees with E. M. Forster that he 'is not a figure of fun'; but he concludes that in his pessimism 'certainly he is Mrs Ramsay's opposite'.[16] Turning to the text to see who makes that pronouncement, we discover that it is Mrs Ramsay who says that her husband constantly dwells on the 'most melancholy things' (106). It is she who imagines him harbouring depressing thoughts, groaning and complaining that 'he would have written better books if he had not married'

(106). But these are Mrs Ramsay's thoughts, not his. Moreover, as far as the question of pessimism is concerned, if we stopped to reflect on Mrs Ramsay's dominant mental habit, we would realize that she, more than Mr Ramsay, emerges as the pessimist. It is she who

> had always seized the fact that there is no reason, order, or justice: but suffering, death, the poor. There was no treachery too base for the world to commit; she knew that. No happiness lasted; she knew that (98).

These certainly are not the utterances of an optimist. Thus, his complement she may be; but most assuredly, not his opposite.

In her excellent study, *Virginia Woolf: Her Art as a Novelist*, Joan Bennett, too, makes some highly speculative statements. She says that if, for Mrs Woolf, the typically feminine mind lacks a sense of fact, it is compensated for by 'an especial honesty, an honesty which comes from self-knowledge'. She goes on to say that 'Mrs Ramsay is more honest than her husband. He can be deflected from the truth by vanity, by egotism, even by the distasteful recognition of facts which seem irreconcilable'.[17] But if we turn to the section in which Mrs Ramsay is looking at the Lighthouse, the self-knowledge Mrs Bennett speaks of becomes a little suspect:

> She saw the light again . . . she looked at the steady light, the pitiless, the remorseless, which was so much her, yet so little her . . . (99).

'So much her, yet so little her', indeed, sounds not so much a testament of self-knowledge as it does a veiled confession of the ambivalence she feels about herself, the kind of ambivalence one experiences when one persists (as does Mrs Ramsay) in calling 'life terrible, hostile, and quick to pounce on you if you gave it a chance' (92).

Further on Mrs Bennett, in defending Mrs Ramsay's honesty, writes that she 'will not lie to herself',[18] and then quotes a long passage (presented from Mrs Ramsay's point of view) in which the first paragraph ends with her uttering: 'We are in the hands of the Lord' (97). The second paragraph continues:

> But instantly she was annoyed with herself for saying that. Who had said it? Not she; she had been trapped into saying something she did not mean. She looked up over her knitting and met the third stroke and it seemed to her like her own eyes meeting her own eyes, searching as she alone could search into her mind and heart, purifying out of existence that lie, any lie . . . (97).

Once again, we have to recognize the importance of the angle of narration and remember that this is Mrs Ramsay telling us that she could purify any lie out of existence. And although I do not wish to make an assault on her truthfulness, I think it is important to point out the need for the critic's substantiating such statements with evidence from other fictional sources; that is, from other points of view if he questions, at all, the narrator's reliability. More important than that is to realize that since the character is built cumulatively, a single quotation from an isolated section is seldom sufficient evidence to make a statement convincing. Therefore, I want to emphasize that although Mrs Ramsay may be honest, she intuits a great deal and rarely questions the validity of her intuitions. Lily's account of the way the Rayley's marriage turned out, for example, attests fully to the irony of Mrs Ramsay's intuitive matchmaking.

Thus the problem reduces to one of a narrator's reliability. Mrs Ramsay, for instance, believes that she can purify any lie out of existence; and because she believes it, for her it is true. For the critic (and the reader), however, it need not necessarily be true. His job in a multiple-point-of-view novel is to examine all the angles of view before connecting them in his effort to establish some pattern of meaning. The misjudgments discussed earlier result not only from the critic's nescience of the significance of point of view, but also from an eagerness to attach interpretations to fragments of the work before experiencing the work in its entirety, before sensing its intricate design and the possible meaning or meanings that design may bear.

When Virginia Woolf said to 'record the atoms as they fall upon the mind in the order in which they fall . . . trace the pattern, however disconnected or incoherent in appearance', she was attempting to describe the complex problem she faced in *simulating* the stream of impressions which intrude themselves upon the minds of her characters. In her essay, 'The Mark on the Wall', she demonstrated the technique by recording her own immediate associations. With the 'mark on the wall' as a point of departure, she traces all the associations which colour and enhance each other while simultaneously calling forth new ones; and moving between a hazy past and a shimmering present, she stretches a moment of consciousness into something akin to a hypnotic expansion of time. Eventually she returns to the 'mark on the wall', to the material object which triggered off the cerebral excursion, and sees that 'It was a snail'.

By itself, the essay is an artistically finished piece. But more than that, it is one of the most important expositions of the technique that Virginia Woolf was to use repeatedly and was to develop and refine in presenting the delicate sensibilities of her fictional people.

An extended passage from the third section of the novel will demonstrate the method. Here is Lily Briscoe at her canvas beginning afresh the picture she had attempted ten years earlier. All of these thoughts are hers, taken in sequence:

> With a curious physical sensation, as if she were urged forward and at the same time must hold herself back, she made her first quick decisive stroke. The brush descended. It flickered brown over the white canvas; it left a running

mark. A second time she did it—a third time. And so pausing and so flickering, she attained a dancing rhythmical movement, as if the pauses were one part of the rhythm and the strokes another, and were all related; and so lightly and swiftly pausing, striking, she scored her canvas with brown running nervous lines which had no sooner settled there than they enclosed (she felt it looming out at her) a space. Down in the hollow of one wave she saw the next wave towering higher and higher above her. For what could be more formidable than that space? Here she was again, she thought, stepping back to look at it, drawn out of gossip, out of living, out of community with people into the presence of this formidable ancient enemy of hers—this other thing, this truth, this reality, which suddenly laid hands on her, emerged stark at the back of appearances and commanded her attention. . . .

Then, as if some juice necessary for the lubrication of her faculties were spontaneously squirted, she began precariously dipping among the blues and umbers, moving her brush hither and thither, but it was now heavier and went slower, as if it had fallen in with some rhythm which was dictated to her (she kept looking at the hedge, at the canvas) by what she saw, so that while her hand quivered with life, this rhythm was strong enough to bear her along with it on its current. Certainly she was losing consciousness of outer things. And as she lost consciousness of outer things, and her name and her personality and her appearance, and whether Mr Carmichael was there or not, her mind kept throwing up from its depths, scenes, and names, and sayings, and memories and ideas, like a fountain spurting over that glaring, hideously difficult white space, while she modelled it with greens and blues (235–38).

She remembers Charles Tansley's saying women can't paint, can't write; and this thought carries her back to memories of Mrs Ramsay, to the act of creating, to the meaning of life; she then returns briefly to the material object: Mr Ramsay in the boat, and she recalls Mrs

Ramsay's asking ' "Is it a boat? Is it a cork?" '; and once more she turns reluctantly to her canvas:

> ... Heaven be praised for it, the problem of space remained, she thought, taking up her brush again. It glared at her. The whole mass of the picture was poised upon that weight. Beautiful and bright it should be on the surface, feathery and evanescent, one colour melting into another like the colours on a butterfly's wing; but beneath the fabric must be clamped together with bolts of iron. It was to be a thing you could ruffle with your breath; and a thing you could not dislodge with a team of horses. And she began to lay on a red, a grey, and she began to model her way into the hollow there. At the same time, she seemed to be sitting beside Mrs Ramsay on the beach.
>
> 'Is it a boat? Is it a cask?' Mrs Ramsay said. And she began hunting round for her spectacles. And she sat, having found them, silent, looking out to sea. And Lily, painting steadily, felt as if a door had opened, and one went in and stood gazing silently about in a high cathedral-like place, very dark, very solemn. Shouts came from a world very far away. Steamers vanished in stalks of smoke on the horizon. Charles threw stones and sent them skipping.
>
> Mrs Ramsay sat silent. She was glad, Lily thought, to rest in silence, uncommunicative; to rest in the extreme obscurity of human relationships. Who knows what we are, what we feel? Who knows even at the moment of intimacy. This is Knowledge? Aren't things spoilt then, Mrs Ramsay may have asked (it seemed to have happened so often, this silence by her side) by saying them? Aren't we more expressive thus? The moment at least seemed extraordinarily fertile. She rammed a little hole in the sand and covered it up, by way of burying in it the perfection of the moment. It was like a drop of silver in which one dipped and illumined the darkness of the past (255–56).

And dipping into the paints, she dips again into her memory and collects her impressions of the Rayleys while 'tunnelling her way into her picture, into the past' (258): to the dinner party, to Minta's lost brooch, to Mrs Ramsay's futile attempts to bring about her marriage to Bankes. Then focusing her attention on the drawing-room steps, she feels their extraordinary emptiness:

... For how could one express in words these emotions of the body? express that emptiness there? ... It was one's body feeling, not one's mind. The physical sensations that went with the bare look of the steps had become suddenly extremely unpleasant. To want and not to have, sent up in her body a hardness, a hollowness, a strain. And then to want and not to have—to want and want—how that wrung the heart, and wrung it again and again! Oh, Mrs Ramsay! she called out silently, to that essence which sat by the boat, that abstract one made of her, that woman in grey, as if to abuse her for having gone, and then having gone, come back again. It had seemed so safe, thinking of her. Ghost, air, nothingness, a thing you could play with easily and safely at any time of day or night, she had been that, and then suddenly she put her hand out and wrung the heart thus. Suddenly the empty drawing-room steps, the frill of the chair inside, the puppy tumbling on the terrace, the whole wave and whisper of the garden became like curves and arabesques flourishing round a centre of complete emptiness (265–66).

The emptiness in the picture suddenly becomes the emptiness in herself, her wanting and not having; and her longing for Mrs Ramsay causes tears to erupt. She reflects a little longer and makes several futile attempts at the canvas, when suddenly something happened:

Suddenly the window at which she was looking was whitened by some light stuff behind it. At last then some-body had come into the drawing-room; somebody was sitting in the chair. For Heaven's sake, she prayed, let them sit still there and not come floundering out to talk to her. Mercifully, whoever it was stayed still inside; had settled by some stroke of luck so as to throw an odd-shaped triangular shadow over the step. It altered the composition of the picture a little. It was interesting. It might be useful. Her mood was coming back to her. One must keep on looking without for a second relaxing the intensity of emotion, the determination not to be put off, not to be bamboozled. One must hold the scene—so—in a vice and let nothing come in and spoil it. One wanted, she thought, dipping her brush deliberately, to be on the level of ordinary experience, to feel simply that's a chair, that's a table, and yet at the same time, It's a miracle, it's an ecstasy. The problem might be solved after all. Ah, but what had happened? Some wave of white went over the window pane. The air must have stirred some flounce in the room. Her heart leapt at her and seized her and tortured her.

'Mrs Ramsay! Mrs Ramsay!' she cried, feeling the old horror come back—to want and want and not to have. Could she inflict that still? And then, quietly, as if she refrained, that too became part of ordinary experience, was on a level with the chair, with the table. Mrs Ramsay—it was part of her perfect goodness—sat there quite simply, in the chair, flicked her needles to and fro, knitted her reddish-brown stocking, cast her shadow on the step. There she sat.

. . . Where was that boat now? And Mr Ramsay? She wanted him (299–300).

What we have in these fragments are moments of a consciousness which, having focused on an object of the external world, retreats from it and moves, with great suppleness, from one collateral association to another, until the observing consciousness is far enough from the object so that it can *objectify its associations* before returning to the original object. These passages, so characteristic of Virginia Woolf, essentially involve the interplay between subject and object—the mobilization of cerebral activity that occurs when the mind becomes aware of its own awareness of the objective world.

In dealing with only one angle of vision, we see already how extremely complex the method is—complex because it calls for the delicate balance of being sensitive to the freedom of movement which the thoughts and emotions require, while simultaneously keeping that movement under the strictest intellectual control. That in this novel Mrs Woolf utilizes and modulates nine principal angles of perspective should indicate how intricate the balance must be to keep the experiential life suspended until the design is complete. The two most crucial aspects of the method are recording the *impressions of the moment* and simultaneously rendering the subjective impressions of the manifold consciousnesses—to show their relationships—so that the whole constellation of emotional and mental processes which make up human experience is revealed to the reader.

Because human experience is conceived as an indefinable, continuous and fluid thing, it is important to remember that the impressions do not progress in a logical sequence; rather, they are ordered according to the emotional force of one experiencing consciousness in relation to another. The meaning of life, which Lily Briscoe wants to know, therefore, is not tendered in some 'great revelation'; its meaning comes in 'little daily miracles, illuminations, matches struck unexpectedly in the dark'. Consequently, the reader, always subject to each of the mind's vagaries, begins to see these 'illuminations' as dominant beats in the rhythm of each individual's experience. And from this rhythmic configuration of selected moments, emerges the *shape* within which the *persona* comes to terms with the concrete world and, in dealing with it, comes to know the *quality* of his experience.

'To make of the moment something permanent,' reflects Lily, '—this was the nature of a revelation. In the midst of chaos there is shape' (241). Here is the artist, thinking in terms of painting, what her creator pondered in terms of the novel. The selected moments are essentially selected scenes; and the selected scenes come to life only with particular angles, or combinations of angles, of vision, the choice of which Virginia Woolf came to recognize as she brought her art to its delicate perfection. Her profound awareness of the nature of consciousness provided her with a feeling for the *moment*—that unique stretch of time when the past filters in and saturates the present; when the inner world is projected on and colours the outer; when reflections and impressions of one consciousness unite with or separate from another; when 'this eternal passing and flowing . . . [is] struck into stability' or remains diffuse and disintegrated; when all emotion and sense and past and present and order and disorder and love and hate and joy and sorrow mingle together and give shape to that ineffable experience we call 'living'; and this experience is revealed primarily in Mrs Woolf's arrangement of the minds she chose to mirror their images, ideas, and feelings.

One significant consequence of modulating the manifold perspectives is its effect on the reader. The chapter in which the dinner-party scene (125–68) occurs, for example, is a *tour de force* in the multiple-point-of-view method. Utilizing eight angles of perspective, Mrs Woolf not only created a sequence of startling and often ironic juxtapositions, but also designed a mental hall of mirrors furnished with human emotions, reflections, memories. Like a kaleidoscope being slowly rotated, each piece— each thought, each reverie—slips into its appropriate place to design a poised pattern of stresses and strains, an exquisite balance of human relationships. *But only for the moment.* As the section ends, Mrs Ramsay

> With her foot on the threshold . . . waited a moment longer in a scene which was vanishing even as she looked, and then, as she moved and took Minta's arm and left the room, it changed, it shaped itself differently; it had become, she knew, giving one last look at it over her shoulder, already the past (167–68).

And as the cycle continues, a new design begins to form; and that, too, soon vanishes to make way for another, and still another, until the larger design is complete and the texture, right.

One of the subtle devices which Mrs Woolf uses for *implying* the larger meaning behind small events is effected through the way she juxtaposes her material. For example, on the boat sailing to the lighthouse, as Cam is thinking of James and their compact, a statement within parentheses is interjected, omnisciently: '(and now Macalister's boy had caught a mackerel, and it lay kicking on the floor, with blood on its gills)' (252). Two lines later, we are shifted again into Cam's mind as she watches her father and thinks:

> For no one attracted her more; his hands were beautiful, and his feet, and his voice, and his words, and his haste, and his temper, and his oddity, and his passion, and his saying straight out before every one, we perish, each alone, and his remoteness. . . . But what remained intolerable, she thought, sitting upright, and watching Macalister's boy tug the hook out of the gills of another fish, was that crass blindness and tyranny of his which had poisoned her childhood and raised bitter storms . . . (253).

Shortly following this is Chapter V, presented mainly through Lily Briscoe, which ends with her standing before her easel, crying aloud:

> 'Mrs Ramsay!' . . . 'Mrs Ramsay!' The tears ran down her face.

And immediately, there follows Chapter VI, consisting of two omniscient sentences within brackets:

> [Macalister's boy took one of the fish and cut a square out of its side to bait his hook with. The mutilated body (it was alive still) was thrown back into the sea.]

Had the episode of Macalister's boy and his fish been placed elsewhere, it might have communicated nothing more than the senseless cruelty of adolescence. But surrounded as it is by suggestions of James' antagonism for his father, Mr Ramsay's harshness, Cam's ambivalence, Lily's painful isolation, the passage, through a series of accumulated connotations, takes on a density of meaning, which projects the very stuff of life: the nervous irony of living side by side with irrational hatred, senseless cruelty, physical pain, unrelieved loneliness, irretrievable loss. What is so remarkable is that nowhere does Virginia Woolf communicate this experience in grand scale or with explicit statement. Hers is the subtle and difficult art of patterning.

Instead of a string of dramatic events, the form of the novel is a series of views inside the minds of human beings. And by our very proximity to them, we share their experience of one another and of the world outside. We experience the pattern in which moments of awareness are arranged, so that our interest is sustained not so much by consequences of events—because these are scarcely to be found here—but rather by the way one moment of consciousness enlarges and enriches the other.

We are *not* 'all like Scheherazade's husband'—to oppose E. M. Forster's well-worn phrase—'in that we want to know what happens next'.[19] What we do want to know, however, is how past events or the expectations of possible future events have been or will be experienced by the individual consciousness; *how* each mind feels about what has happened or what is happening or what might happen. Through this progression of inside views, this continual ebb and flow of illumination, our interest is aroused to the extent that we want to continue until the whole tapestry of experience is revealed and felt.

Most readers want, more, to know *how* James Ramsay will experience the Lighthouse when the expedition is finally made than to know the simple fact that the expedition *is* made. And having carefully prepared us throughout the novel for this moment, Mrs Woolf gives us a vibrant picture of that consciousness feeling something for the first time in all its freshness and vitality and truth:

The Lighthouse was then a silvery, misty-looking tower with a yellow eye, that opened suddenly, and softly in the evening. Now—

James looked at the Lighthouse. He could see the whitewashed rocks; the tower, stark and straight; he could see that it was barred with black and white; he could see windows in it; he could even see washing spread on the rocks to dry. So that was the Lighthouse, was it?

No, the other was also the Lighthouse. For nothing was simply one thing. The other Lighthouse was true too . . . (276–77).

Because Virginia Woolf saw the human personality shaped by the 'shower of atoms' that strike upon its consciousness, she was to create moments of heightened awareness, when the mind is quickened to see order in chaos. Her whole gallery of characters, their impressions myriad and divers, shuttling between past and present, are all modulated to the service of making that heightened moment permanent.

Like E. M. Forster, Elizabeth Drew wants things to happen in the novel and criticizes *To the Lighthouse* for its

lack of any progressive action involving moral and emotional choices and decisions. . . . We see very clearly what the characters have made of them [their lives], but they are forced to remain static; it is all expansion without progression.[20]

Since 'expansion' implies space and 'progression' time, we might recall Flaubert's 'comice agricole' scene in *Madame Bovary* to see what spatialization of form means in the novel. I refer to Flaubert's experiment here because Virginia Woolf, in a considerably more sophisticated way, has accomplished essentially the same thing in rendering aesthetically the simultaneity of the moment. When her narrator embarks on a mental excursion of associations, Mrs Woolf brings clock time in the narrative to a halt: the horizontal progression of time ceases; and a vertical expansion of psychological time takes over in that limited time-area; during that time the character, seemingly in cerebral isolation, not only communicates the quality of his experience but also partially reveals himself. When mechanical time ceases, then, and experiential time expands, independent of the novel's temporal progress, it becomes clear that the significance of any one moment can be understood only in its reflexive relationship to the numerous other moments to which it makes reference. Speaking of *Ulysses*, Joseph Frank asserted that 'these references must be connected by the reader and viewed as a whole before the book fits together in any meaningful pattern'.[21] We have only to re-read the third part of Mrs Woolf's novel to see how dependent it is on the first section for its effect. Lily Briscoe's reveries, in particular, derive their integrative power by the very nature of their reflexive relations to the references of all the principal angles of perspective introduced in the first part of the novel.

The way these points of view have been ordered to make the structure—the formal relations of the manifold consciousnesses—communicates the meaning of the work. As I indicated earlier, no single meaning can ever be ascribed to a great work of art. Part of its enduring quality is in its meaning different things to different people at different times. Therefore the interpretation at which I will eventually arrive results primarily from a consideration of the sequence and manipulation of multiple perspectives as a critical approach; and as such it is merely a demonstration of how that approach works.

*   *   *

If we look to see how the perspectives are distributed throughout the novel, we will discover that each of its three sections is dominated by a single consciousness; that is, almost fifty per cent of Part I is transmitted through Mrs Ramsay, more than seventy-five per cent of Part II through the Omniscient Narrator, and more than sixty per cent of Part III is presented through Lily Briscoe. By themselves, these figures might be interesting; however they are worthless unless we discern the thematic content as well as the emotional quality and consistency of each section.

Critics generally agree that on the prose plane the novel deals with female intuition and male intellection; permanence and change; order and chaos; the art of living and the life of art. But critical consensus vanishes immediately an attempt is made to follow through these themes.

From even a brief perusal of the critical literature, what emerges is the tendency to abstract the conflict into two mutually exclusive phenomena: either permanence or change; either intuition or intellection; either order or chaos; and so on. To see the disparate, the contradictory elements, and to be unaware of their reconcilability is to miss the interpretive framework which, in fact, embraces these pervasive opposites. *That Virginia Woolf should have chosen to use multiple perspectives is indication enough that no interpretation can be arrived at which settles on one aspect at the expense of the other.*

Fundamentally, the problem is, as Norman Friedman[22] suggested, one of relations: the relationship between one individual and another, between man and nature, and between life and art. For Virginia Woolf, the basic resolution to this duality was in understanding the relationship between the opposites and in apprehending their essential congruity. For her, this was the nature of reality: not 'either . . . or', but 'both'. James, for example, begins to mature when he realizes that 'the other was also the Lighthouse. For nothing was simply one thing' (277). The

novel is rife with suggestions of contradictory yet recon-
cilable elements. And structurally it is built along those
lines.

Part I, made up of seventeen angles of perspective,
amply demonstrates the complexity of the relationship
between one individual and another, with no single
character emerging as a set personality. The traits which
define him] and instil in him a recognizable reality come
with repeated shifts in the multiple-consciousness design.
A character is revealed not only from his interior mono-
logues, but also from the impressions he elicits from
others. It becomes clear, as the section progresses, that
each narrator is made up of numerous contradictory
ingredients. Mrs Ramsay, for instance, maternal, gener-
ous, and loving as she is, is also a meddling, self-seeking,
possessive affection-monger. To see only her flattering
qualities and to ignore the rest is to miss entirely the
truth of her personality and the significance of her por-
trayal.

Mr Ramsay, too, for all his intellectual sternness and
domestic tyranny, is an admirably unworldly man;
austerely philosophical, yet actively engaged with home
and family; grimly aware of the dark of human ignorance,
yet optimistic in the face of life's other realities; insensitive
to the texture of a rose petal, yet keenly aware of his wife's
subtle changes of temper.

William Bankes is a man dedicated to the large concerns of science, yet irritable and picayune in his dietary
fads; a gentleman of poise who respects old friends, he is
nevertheless frustrated in his affections and occasionally
insincere in his friendships. Charles Tansley is an irritat-
ing, egocentric bundle of rudeness and inferiority, yet is
a sympathetic human being for whom, as Mrs Ramsay
says, 'success would be good'. There is also Lily Briscoe,
surely a complex figure of opposing tendencies: a spinster
who shies away from intense human attachments, yet
capable of anguished eruptions of love; a modest painter
frightened of the obstacles imposed by her craft, yet brave

and determined enough to wrestle with the problems and eventually to overcome them.

In Part I, dominated by Mrs Ramsay, by means of shifting perspectives, the inconsistencies in the characters are exposed, and the difficulty in their relationships is revealed. It is also here that the chaos of their relations is momentarily and superficially resolved into order through Mrs Ramsay's efforts at the dinner party, which climaxes this section of the novel.

Part II, given primarily through the Omniscient Narrator, is a short poetic interlude dealing metaphysically with man's relation to nature. A sense of loss and change and frustration pervades the first half of the section: Mrs Ramsay dies; Andrew is killed in France; Prue dies in childbed; the house and everything in it are near total ruin. The destructive forces of the natural world are dramatized; but equally dramatic is the human capacity to check and finally to defeat those chaotic energies through a stronger force—the will to endure. As though some miraculous human strength were mobilized, there follows a dramatic renascence of all that has been ravaged.

It is symptomatic that this middle section is not presented through the intuitive imagination of a Mrs Ramsay or the artistic sensibility of a Lily Briscoe. Although the 'willing suspension of disbelief' is interrupted, causing the reader to re-adjust to a distance considerably removed from the scene, the inevitable passage of time, presented as it is, not only enhances our sense of the capricious whirlwinds of time and nature but also serves to make the necessary separation between Mrs Ramsay and Lily Briscoe a function in the total effect of the novel's design.

Part III centres on the relationship of art to life, and Lily Briscoe is its governing consciousness. In the boat Mr Ramsay, James, and Cam are struggling with the problem of human relations, while on shore Lily is struggling with the problem of the formal relations in her picture. She grapples with her canvas while simultaneously reviving the image she has of Mrs Ramsay; and it is only when she feels the need to see life 'on a level with ordinary experience', to see something as it is and at the same time as a 'miracle', an 'ecstasy', that she begins to see the real Mrs Ramsay underneath that superficial beauty; and with that she feels a sudden upsurge of sympathy for Mr Ramsay—something she had been incapable of feeling before. She begins to fathom the Ramsay's relationship as husband and wife, an understanding which bears with it a clearer grasp of the art of human relations—something she had not understood before.

While these moments of illumination are occurring on shore, long since disturbed relations are being resolved on the trip to the Lighthouse: Cam's antagonism for her father vanishes; James' hatred disappears with his father's words of praise. Mr Ramsay's anxieties are being resolved. Integrity in the family is finally being realized. And running parallel with it is Lily's final apprehension that in harmonious human relations there is a deep involvement in life; she realizes that for the artist such involvement is necessary before he can become objectively detached from it to seize its harmony and translate it into the aesthetic relations of art. Only when she grasps these strange entanglements of human intercourse can she complete herself as a human being and fulfil herself as an artist. For art and life are no longer hostile to each other; and one can not be objectively detached from the former without first being subjectively involved with the latter. Only with this realization can she feel simply that 'that's a chair . . . yet, at the same time, It's a miracle. . . .' This duality of vision is essential to her understanding of the nature of reality. Lily comes to know, what Mrs Ramsay had always thought she, herself, knew intuitively: that with simultaneous involvement and detachment, art, like life, can be shaped and moulded. And in her wanting Mr Ramsay, Lily begins to see what is necessary for the achievement of 'that razor edge of balance between two opposite forces: Mr Ramsay [involvement] and the picture [detachment]' (287).

On the prose plane, then, this is how the novel organizes both in terms of its formal divisions and its distribution and modulation of the manifold consciousnesses. The fabric of the literary experience is spun between the minds of the *personae* and our grasp of what and how they feel in their relationship to one another and to their experience of reality. The singular excellence of *To the Lighthouse* originates in Virginia Woolf's seeing the problem and dealing with it in terms of the inner states of multiple human consciousnesses.

The novel, however, also operates on the plane of poetry. On that plane, language, heightened by various poetic devices, is the basic instrument informing the work's intensity and integrity and authority. The novel does not progress on the 'what-happens-next' basis. Rather it moves forward on the arrangement of scenes, on the sequence of selected moments of consciousness.

If we are alert to the imagery, frequently we will see images, as simile or metaphor, gradually acquiring symbolic dimension. Once the symbol is established, it is often possible to trace the novel's narrative progress in terms of that symbol's extension and expansion. By moving into the province of poetry, Virginia Woolf was able to overcome many of the difficulties indigenous to prose expression. As she wrote in her essay on Montaigne:

> Face, voice, and accent eke out our words and impress their feebleness with character in speech. But the pen is a rigid instrument; it can say very little. . . .[23]

An attempt to trace the imagery and determine its use in a work so freighted with images is by itself the basis for a full-length study. An example or two will suffice, to show how an image grows to symbolic potential, while carrying the narrative forward; and how poetic connotations accrue which define the terms upon which the novel's meaning rests.

Mrs Woolf's nineteen direct references to the 'hedge', for example, although an inconspicuous image, are indeed illustrative.[24] It is introduced for the first time on page 32, with Lily Briscoe's:

> 'I'm in love with this all,' waving her hands at the hedge, at the house, at the children.

After three more references, it is brought up by Mr Ramsay on page 56 when he meditates on the endurance of fame. He guesses that it lasts perhaps two thousand years.

> And what are two thousand years? (asked Mr Ramsay ironically, staring at the hedge). . . . His own little light would shine, not very brightly, for a year or two. . . . (He looked into the hedge, into the intricacy of the twigs.)

Mentioned parenthetically, the seemingly irrelevant reference to the hedge is brought up again on page 66 when Mr Ramsay stops and watches his wife reading to James the story of the Fisherman and his wife (the story, incidentally, in this context is extremely revealing, because it is analogous to the very marital conflict which exists between Mr and Mrs Ramsay):

> Mrs Ramsay could have wished that her husband had not chosen that moment to stop. . . . But he did not speak; he looked; he nodded; he approved; he went on. He slipped, seeing before him that hedge which had over and over again rounded some pause, signified some conclusion, seeing his wife and child. . . .

Fifteen pages later, Lily Briscoe, now as the centre of consciousness, takes up the image.[25] When Bankes asks about her painting, she finds herself

> becoming once more under the power of that vision which she had seen clearly once and must now grope for among hedges and houses and mothers and children—her picture (82).

Later still we find Mr Ramsay looking at his wife, withdrawn to her 'wedge of darkness', deep in thought as she watches the strokes of the Lighthouse:

> It saddened him, and her remoteness pained him, and he felt, as he passed, that he could not protect her, and, when he reached the hedge, he was sad. He could do nothing to help her. . . . He looked into the hedge, into its intricacy, its darkness . . . (98–99).

The hedge begins to enlarge in its suggestive powers as its contexts become more particularized. However, it is not mentioned again until the last movement of the novel when Lily pitches her easel precisely where

> she had stood ten years ago. There was the wall; the hedge; the tree. The question was of some relation between those masses (221).

She stands poised with brush in hand and 'looked at the hedge, the step, the wall' and thinks ironically: 'It was all Mrs Ramsay's doing' (223). She reflects back on the first attempt to paint her picture and remembered something

> in the relations of those lines cutting across, slicing down, and in the mass of the hedge with its green cave of blues and browns . . . (234).

And she continues to grapple with her aesthetic problem, constantly

> looking at the hedge, at the canvas (237).

As she ponders Mrs Ramsay and surrenders to a fierce outburst of loneliness, she approaches part of the solution which drives her to attack again

> that problem of the hedge (269).

Still something evaded her, something in the human apparatus that broke down at the critical moment; heroically, one must force it on. She stared, frowning. There was the hedge, sure enough. But one got nothing by soliciting urgently. One got only a glare in the eye from looking at the line of the wall, or from thinking—she wore a grey hat. She was astonishingly beautiful (287–88).

These repeated juxtapositions of the hedge and Mrs Ramsay begin now to assume great significance. For Virginia Woolf is no longer talking about a hedge, it is clear, but rather about a barrier, a psychic blockade, an emotional wall. And as such, the 'hedge' is now functioning as an ever-enlarging symbol.

Lily continues to wonder about Mrs Ramsay. She wants to know

her thoughts, her imaginations, her desires. What did the hedge mean to her . . . (294).

And at last,

There it was—her picture. Yes, with all its greens and blues, its lines running up and across, its attempt at something (309).[26]

Lily has finally understood the real Mrs Ramsay, the barrier in the relationship between husband and wife, and between father and son; and she no longer wants her. Now it is Mr Ramsay she wants: he is now the positive force.

As the boat moves farther and farther away, Lily gets nearer to understanding and overcoming the complexity of her problem, her artistic vision approaching ever more closely its aesthetic integrity. The instinctive need for distance—that necessary objectivity for the artist—is finally being realized; and her involvement in life begins to take on the permanence of truth: '. . . so much depends, she thought, on distance: whether people are near us or far from us . . .' (284). From that distance Lily now sees Mrs Ramsay with that one pair of eyes among fifty 'that was stone blind to her beauty'. As she subdues her involvement and increases her detachment to that razor-edge of balance, she is able, at last, to seize the fluidity of life and strike it into the stable reality of art.

Thus the hedge, in the beginning generalized and seemingly irrelevant, begins to grow, with repetition and with varied contexts, to symbolic dimensions; and parallel to its growth runs the narrative progression of the novel. Thus what is of central significance to the meaning of the work is handled, in part, through this symbol—deceptively slight though it seems.

Other isolated symbols refer to the basic concept of the work, such as the green shawl, the pig's skull, the colours of Lily's paints, the story of the Fisherman and his Wife, to name but a few. But the symbol having the most uncircumscribed power of suggestion is the Lighthouse, itself. Because 'the more barren and indifferent the symbol, the greater its semantic power',[27] the Lighthouse means different things to different readers. It seems appropriate that we approach it in its most general terms as a structure representing the concept of a goal: a fulfilment of some sort; something to be reached; a quest involving an elaborate pattern of relations.

The Lighthouse, on the novel's poetic plane, is a source of light which does not become a source of illumination until after Mrs Ramsay's death. Thus, we might conceive of it as the goal of creating lasting harmony from the chaos of inadequate human relationships. The expedition to the Lighthouse is introduced on the first page; and its mention also introduces a conflict between husband and wife, a disturbance in the relations between father and son, and later Mrs Ramsay's domination over husband and family.

In the first section of the work, governed by Mrs Ramsay's point of view, the Lighthouse as a symbol of the goal of human harmony is ironic, because the expedition to the Lighthouse becomes a frustrated goal; and the harmony Mrs Ramsay effects is superficial and short-lived (the Rayley's marriage, Lily's spinsterhood, James' Oedipean problem). In this section we see not the Lighthouse but only its light—and that, only mistily through Mrs Ramsay's 'short-sighted eyes' (109), when she is withdrawn from the human community to her 'wedge of darkness'. Her association with the Lighthouse reveals all her remoteness and estrangement and selfhood. It reveals as well the contradictory forces she represents in not attaining any real human attachments: in not going beyond her self to an other-centred world of human communion. Paradoxically, her involvement in life is, for the most part, objective: it is a means of placing herself at the centre—yet without being part—of the human fanfare that clutters her existence. Equally paradoxical is her detachment, because it is subjective: she withdraws to avoid seeing her own inadequacies, to reflect upon her attributes and life's cruelties and hardships, to absolve herself of real or imagined guilt. That is, she withdraws in a gesture of self-protection.

In the early part of the second section, the light appears again. This time it illuminates the indifference of nature to man's creation as seen in the destruction of the house and those things meaningful to the Ramsay family. The stroke is a gentle, caressing one. And just before the house is to be resurrected, the beam stares, undisturbed, at the 'thistle and the swallow, the rat and the straw. Nothing now withstood them; nothing said no to them' (208).

In this lyrical middle section, governed by the Omniscient Narrator, we begin to sense the connection between the Lighthouse and one's relations to others and between the Lighthouse and nature's indifference to human life. Its suggestiveness, as an unfixed symbol, increases as the novel unfolds. But more than that, as its contexts multiply and vary, the Lighthouse—by symbolic extension—carries the narrative forward, since as a goal the structure itself has not been reached.

In the third section, the expedition is made; and as the boat approaches the Lighthouse, the problem of harmony approaches resolution: Cam comes to terms with her father; James, at last, has found a father; and Mr Ramsay becomes, finally, the respected head of the family, he has been fulfilled as a father—something which, during Mrs Ramsay's life, was impossible.

By no means do I wish to insinuate that Mrs Ramsay is to be condemned entirely or that Mr Ramsay is to be wholly exonerated: both are flawed. Mr Ramsay, for example, in addressing Cam, still reveals his austere and uncompromising dedication to fact:

> for he could not understand the state of mind of any one, not absolutely imbecile, who did not know the points of the compass. Yet she did not know (249).

Nor do I wish to insinuate that James' finding a father is the proper conclusion of the book. What I do want to suggest is that by James' final emotional alignment with his father, he has matured; and his new maturity is revealed in his ability to view opposites simultaneously that is, now he sees the Lighthouse not only as his mother once hazily saw it—'a silvery, misty-looking tower with a yellow eye . . .'—but also as his father clearly sees it— 'the tower, stark and straight . . . barred with black and white. . . .' In his seeing both images of the Lighthouse as being true, like his sister Cam who already understands this double vision, he has grown to that level of maturity which sees life's antitheses in reconciliatory terms. And it is precisely because of the prerequisite self-integrating power of this double vision, that real integration, among these human beings at the Lighthouse, has been achieved.

On shore, Lily Briscoe is simultaneously approaching a resolution to her problem of aesthetic relationships. For as the distance between her and Mr Ramsay increases, she gains a new perspective which puts Mrs Ramsay into proper focus: Mrs Ramsay is now the dark mass. Seeing her, Lily's hitherto withheld sympathy for Mr Ramsay is released. Now she too, having experienced subjective involvement, can see clearly enough to detach herself

objectively and see the integration her painting requires
—an integration effected by a single line 'there, in the
centre' (310). That line, almost certainly, refers to the
Lighthouse: the symbolic goal of human harmony
prerequisite to the achievement of artistic integrity.

It was Mrs Ramsay who suggested the trip, and it is
Mr Ramsay who finally makes it; it was Mrs Ramsey
whom Lily worshipped and Mr Ramsay who now com-
mands her vision. And strongly implied here is the idea
that real harmony—whether on the human plane or on the
aesthetic—could not be achieved until after Mrs Ramsay's
death. It is thus possible to see how on both the literal and
symbolic levels—the prose and poetic planes—the novel,
in its most general meaning, organizes around the need
for both human involvement and artistic detachment
in life, which is the very centre of art. Only then does
that mysterious principle effect the proper relationships
which reveal the complex nature of reality and at the same
time realize, aesthetically, the chaotic reality of nature.

Chapter Six

A STYLISTIC ANALYSIS
OF THE NOVEL

WHEN dealing with a work such as *To the Lighthouse* in which the mental contents of the narrators are presented to the reader without auctorial mediation—as, for example, interior monologue which generally does not resemble the linguistic organizations of public discourse—the problem arises as to which grammar will best identify and describe the structural components of the utterances. Despite the present inchoate state of English descriptive grammar and the fact that grammatical and semantic categories (as well as grammatical and logical categories) do not always coincide, those works, most useful in clarifying structural ambiguities and making possible at least analytical consistency, were Zellig S. Harris' *Methods in Structural Linguistics* (1951), Charles C. Fries' *The Structure of English* (1952), Noam A. Chomsky's *Syntactic Structures* (1957), James Sledd's *A Short Introduction to English Grammar* (1959), and Robert B. Lees' *The Grammar of English Nominalizations* (1960).

Although these became the ultimate authority for determining grammatical classes and distinctions, I have used the terminology of traditional grammar throughout the study for at least three reasons. First, traditional labels are likely to be understood by more readers: even today, most teachers of English and literary critics will recognize 'word' and not 'morpheme', 'adjective' and not 'class 3 word', 'noun' and not 'nominal', and so on. Second, although kernel sentences and transformations are central concepts in Generative grammar, there is, at present, still no general agreement among the Generativists as to what constitutes the truest kernels (or the transforms of kernels); and this has led to some confusion in their terminology with respect to adjectival modifiers, determiners, and possessives, for example. Lastly, and most important, when Generative grammarians deal with anything beyond the simplest matters of analysis, their terminology becomes so burdened with difficult jargon that few readers are likely to take the trouble of decoding it.

I

The term 'sentence' here refers to that word or series of words which begins with a capital letter and ends with a terminal punctuation mark (period, question mark, exclamation mark, dash, or ellipsis).[1] Because the sentence is the primary unit of understanding, and because interpretation of any literary work must begin by apprehending each of these units—one by one, in their sequence—my initial aim in examining these Woolf samples (see Appendix A) was to see how much variation the sentences revealed in length and in their clausal components, and how much clausal embedding there was in each of the specimens. The effort was to determine whether these stylistic features differed sufficiently from one narrator to the next to be considered cues functioning to aid the reader in distinguishing between the narrators in a multiple-point-of-view novel such as *To the Lighthouse*.

Moreover, by isolating the constituents of the sentences, especially on the clausal level, I was better able to describe those syntactic arrangements to which the reader habitually responds in organizing his own experiences—responses which those syntactic organizations encourage. In short, it was possible to examine in more scientific terms those micro-rhetorical features of language which influence the semantic substance of any utterance.

Although many significant features of Virginia Woolf's prose style have already been discussed in considerable detail and although some points may be repeated for emphasis, my main purpose here is to supplement the qualitative judgments made earlier in the critical reading of the novel, by comparing the over-all quantitative values.

If we look first at the number of sentences and the length variations, we see immediately that there are no dramatic differences; that is, differences so evident that

Table 1

Narrator	Number of Sentences	Mean Sentence Length (in Syllables)	Standard Deviation of Sentence Length (in Syllables)
Mrs Ramsay	58	19·12	17·71
Mr Ramsay	36	30·89	31·59
James Ramsay	40	26·73	24·67
Cam Ramsay	40	26·93	22·29
Omniscient	30	38·27	25·96
William Bankes	53	21·28	21·40
Charles Tansley	53	20·42	24·57
Lily Briscoe	36	32·14	33·74
Mrs McNab	68	15·22	13·22

they could not be ignored. Yet differences, subtle as they are, do exist; and from them several important observations can be made. Looking down the first column of values, we note that Mr Ramsay, the Omniscient Narrator, and Lily Briscoe have the lowest number of sentences; that James and Cam are identical in this aspect, as are William Bankes and Charles Tansley; and that Mrs McNab has the highest number. As a consequence of the first observation, the mean lengths of the sentences of Mr Ramsay, the Omniscient Narrator, and Lily are the highest in numerical value; again, for James and Cam, they are almost identical; and for Mrs McNab, the value is lowest. With respect to sentence length variation *within* each of the samples, we see that Mr Ramsay's and Lily's sentences have the greatest variety, and that Mrs McNab's (followed closely in value by Mrs Ramsay's) sentences are the least varied.

It should be pointed out that tests of *statistical signifi-cance* such as 'Chi-Square' or 'Analysis of Variance' (see Appendix B) were not used here for the more specific stylistic dimensions examined; and the reason should be obvious: if, for example, it were found that the differences in mean sentence length between Mr Ramsay (30·89) and Lily Briscoe (32·14) or that the differences between the standard deviations of James Ramsay (24·67) and the Omniscient Narrator (25·96) were statistically significant on the 0·01 or the 0·05 level of confidence, that information would be meaningless because the differences would be significant for the statistician—but *not* necessarily for the reader. In other words, the differences, whether statisti-cally significant or not, would have no meaning for the reader because they are not substantively different in value. And since I am concerned with *substantive differences*, unless quantitative values for the various narrators are dramati-cally different from one another, they will not be considered stylistic features which help the reader to distinguish between the narrators, but rather stylistic habits which characterize the author's prose in general—and, as such, are not of great importance to the analysis of the multiple-point-of-view novel.

It would be difficult to determine whether the differ-ences in the three items of Table 2 are both statistically *and substantively* significant. However, one could speculate, with a reasonably high degree of confidence, that if a reader came to a section narrated by the Omniscient Narrator or Lily Briscoe, for example, and then read a section narrated by Mrs McNab, he would immediately sense a stylistic difference; whereas if he came to sections narrated by James and Cam (discounting the content of their utterance), he would have considerable difficulty in differentiating between the two. In other words, Virginia Woolf tends to blur differences between some narrators, while making others fairly distinct, stylistically.[2]

On the clausal level, the sentences are made up of the following:

Table 2

Narrator	No. Clauses	Main	Adverb	Adjective	Noun	Parenthetical
Mrs Ramsay	103	65	14	7	16	1
		63%	14%	7%	16%	<1%
Mr Ramsay	82	46	17	11	8	—
		56%	21%	13%	10%	—
James Ramsay	99	57	10	11	17	4
		58%	10%	11%	17%	4%
Cam Ramsay	106	51	12	6	33	4
		48%	11%	6%	31%	4%
Omniscient	76	40	10	8	16	2
		53%	13%	11%	21%	2%
William Bankes	108	59	12	7	32	2
		54%	11%	6%	29%	<1%
Charles Tansley	111	64	4	10	31	2
		58%	4%	9%	28%	1%
Lily Briscoe	92	48	7	11	17	9
		50%	8%	12%	18%	12%
Mrs McNab	101	76	11	2	7	5
		75%	11%	2%	7%	5%

With regard to clause number, again only Mr Ramsay, the Omniscient Narrator, and Lily Briscoe appear appreciably to differ from the others; and with regard to main clauses, Mrs McNab's percentage is substantially different—that is, of all the narrators, her utterances contain the least modification, her thoughts the least amplification. In so far as adverbial, adjectival, and parenthetical (in this last category, possibly with the exception of Lily) clauses are concerned, there seems to be nothing remarkable either in the range of differences or in the variation of percentages.

The evaluations ascribed to the noun clauses, however, require some explanation, because Virginia Woolf not only constantly shifts the angles of perspective, but also constantly shifts between the techniques of direct and indirect interior monologue; this means that she must use such markers as 'thought Lily' or 'she remembered . . .' or 'James said', in order to signal the reader as to which consciousness the material is being filtered through. For the stylistic analyst this presents a problem, because quite often a sample begins with a sentence in which a 'he thought' marker is buried; and as a consequence all subsequent clauses, which would otherwise be counted as main, now become noun clauses. A further complication arises when, in the separate sentences following the first, containing the 'he thought' marker, we essentially have a sequence of separate thoughts which should likewise be called noun clauses. However, a brief perusal of the samples in Appendix A will indicate that rarely—in fact, never—is it possible to say where one series of thoughts ends and another begins: that is, whether the thoughts should be counted as main clauses or as noun clauses. Stated in another way, it is rarely possible to say whether Mrs Woolf intended a thought to be presented as *indirect* interior monologue, which would make it a noun clause, and those following (but without the marker) also noun clauses; or whether she meant those thoughts following to be presented technically as *direct* interior monologue, which would require classifying them as main clauses.

One might argue that 'he thought' properly belongs to the omniscient author; and, strictly speaking, that is true. However, because direct and indirect interior monologue are so subtly and inextricably interwoven, in order to avoid questionable guesswork, a thought, whenever it appeared as a complete sentence without the 'he thought' marker, was invariably considered a main clause. In this way only could consistency be maintained from one sentence to another and from one sample to the next. Moreover, had the 'he thought' markers been eliminated from the samples altogether, the main and noun clause counts would have yielded different numerical data. This fact notwithstanding, the *relative* frequencies of the narrators' clause counts would remain absolutely unaltered.

Differences in the quantities of clausal components merely describe in objective measurements the various kinds of modification which generate a narrator's sentences. But linguistic science does not yet offer an extensive, systematic body of information which goes beyond description to interpretation. However, another important stylistic feature on the level of the sentence may be profitably analysed; and that is the amount of clause embedding found in the individual samples. Specifically, it is the determination of the ratio of rates of occurrence of main clauses to the ratio of rates of occurrence of embedded clauses (the total number of dependent clauses). As Richard Ohmann[3] pointed out, the greater the amount of embedded elements in relation to the main sentence itself, the greater the difficulty in grasping the ideas, because of the strain put on the reader's attention and the memory required to follow the progress of the sentence. From the percentages below,

Table 3

Narrator	Main Clauses	Embedded Clauses	Ratio of Rates: Main Clauses / Embedded Clauses
Mrs Ramsay	65	38	171%
Mr Ramsay	46	36	128%
James Ramsay	57	42	136%
Cam Ramsay	51	55	93%
Omniscient	40	36	111%
William Bankes	59	53	111%
Charles Tansley	64	47	136%
Lily Briscoe	48	44	109%
Mrs McNab	76	25	304%

at least two observations can be made. That Mrs McNab differs so sharply from the others implies that Mrs Woolf must have meant to distinguish the language of the Irish charwoman from that of the more refined sensibilities and more mature language of the other narrators. With perhaps the exception of Mrs Ramsay, there seems to be no deliberate effort to distinguish the narrators from one another on the basis of main and embedded clause ratios.

II

In the vocabulary analysis, some expectations are violated, others are not. The values in the table below in

Table 4

Narrator	Mean Word Length (in Syllables)	Nouns with Latin Suffixes	Latin-Derived Verbs	Content Words	Structural[4] Words
Mrs Ramsay	1·32	10 + 7 = 17		34%	66%
Mr Ramsay	1·32	23 + 11 = 34		35%	65%
James Ramsay	1·37	9 + 12 = 21		36%	64%
Cam Ramsay	1·28	5 + 10 = 15		37%	63%
Omniscient	1·37	15 + 27 = 42		56%	44%
William Bankes	1·35	29 + 21 = 50		36%	64%
Charles Tansley	1·29	4 + 12 = 16		34%	66%
Lily Briscoe	1·38	9 + 19 = 28		39%	61%
Mrs McNab	1·23	4 + 7 = 11		36%	64%

the 'mean-word-length' column, for example, reveal no remarkable differences between the narrators; and while more substantial contrasts would have emerged had the word-length counts been made after separating the one-, two-, three-, four-, and five-syllable words, it bears repeating that the analyst may sense differences from such separation; but the general reader does not: his impression is formed by the words taken as a whole. Thus we can say, only, that although the differences are greatly depressed, the reader probably feels the brevity of Mrs McNab's vocabulary, as opposed to the increased word lengths of Lily Briscoe, the Omniscient narrator, and William Bankes.

The values of the second column are consonant with the image we have of each narrator and consistent with the critical sketches made in Chapter Five. For example, the vocabularies respectively of William Bankes, the Omniscient Narrator, Mr Ramsay (and perhaps Lily Briscoe) are substantially more Latinate than the others, which indicates their greater linguistic command and mental cultivation. By contrast, the relatively low use of Latinate words is appropriate for Mrs Ramsay who intuits life and recoils from intellection; for James and Cam who are youthful and not yet linguistically sophisticated; for Charles Tansley who merely aspires to the intellectual world; and for Mrs McNab, whose interests in life have nothing to do with either linguistic refinement or anything else beyond the most ordinary.

In so far as the percentages of Content and Structural Words are concerned, no appreciable differences exist, with the exception of the Omniscient Narrator whose use of idea- and image-bearing words far exceeds that of the other narrators; and it takes no systematic analysis of style to discover how extraordinarily rich his prose is in both texture and substance.

III

Verb density is another stylistic dimension which can be useful for differentiating the narrator. It is determined by calculating the ratio of the rates of occurrence of verbals (participles,[5] gerunds, and infinitives) to the ratio of the rates of occurrence of finite verbs. Since verbals do not take subjects, and finite verbs do, it is logical to assume that the higher the percentage of verbals in relation to finite verbs, the less structured the language and, consequently, the more difficult to follow. Although from the ratio of percentages listed in the following table, one might infer that Tansley's utterances (29%) are the most organized and the clearest in meaning, and that Mr Ramsay's (42%) are the least, there is neither a statistically nor a substantively significant difference to support

Table 5

Narrator	$Participles$ + $Gerunds$ + $Infinitives$ = Verbals	Finite Verbs	Ratio of Rates: Verbals / Finite Verbs
Mrs Ramsay	17 + 8 + 19 = 44	114	39%
Mr Ramsay	22 + 3 + 13 = 38	90	42%
James Ramsay	20 + 4 + 11 = 35	109	32%
Cam Ramsay	27 + 2 + 12 = 41	113	36%
Omniscient	37 + 1 + 2 = 40	109	37%
William Bankes	23 + 2 + 14 = 38	112	34%
Charles Tansley	14 + 3 + 20 = 37	128	29%
Lily Briscoe	30 + 2 + 11 = 43	114	38%
Mrs McNab	19 + 2 + 17 = 38	114	33%

the inference. Actually the mean for all the narrators is 36·5%, and no deviation exceeds 6·5%. Thus, we can say that Mrs Woolf does not attempt to distinguish one narrator from another on the basis of this stylistic feature; but rather, she tends to *obscure* differences by keeping the very density fairly constant for all the narrators, including Mrs McNab.

IV

Personal affect is an area of analysis adapted from John B. Carroll's *Vectors of Prose Style*[6] and is intended to provide evidence of the extent to which a narrator is presented sympathetically to the reader. Put another way, it is the extent to which an author effects, linguistically, various degrees of distance between the reader and the narrator. Sympathy, according to Carroll, is created when the tone of the prose is personal and intimate. He found that samples of writing, judged to be personal and intimate, contained a low number of syllables (relatively short words), a high percentage of cognitive verbs (verbs of thinking, feeling, and believing), a low number of common nouns, and a large number of pronouns with a high proportion of personal pronouns. The data reveal only

Table 6

Narrator	No. Syllables	Cognitive Verbs	No. Common Nouns	No. Personal Pronouns	No. Pronouns
Mrs Ramsay	1109	9%	130	99	121
Mr Ramsay	1112	4%	139	64	91
James Ramsay	1069	12%	131	65	95
Cam Ramsay	1078	13%	123	90	116
Omniscient	1148	1%	180	40	63
William Bankes	1138	20%	130	74	106
Charles Tansley	1082	13%	119	112	138
Lily Briscoe	1157	9%	126	75	103
Mrs McNab	1035	10%	140	89	110

that the Omniscient Narrator might be considered the least personal, the most remote. As for the other items counted, however, no significant substantive differences were discovered from one narrator to the next.

However, although no appreciable inequalities were found, it is necessary to remember that in a multiple-point-of-view novel, in impersonal narration, the author must make each of his narrators engaging in varying degrees if he wishes to succeed in getting the reader actively to participate in the work. And if we recall that in this novel even Charles Tansley, for example, is capable of evoking some very sympathetic responses from the reader, then we realize that there had to be an equality of personal affect (with the exception of the Omniscient Narrator) if Mrs Woolf was to succeed in involving her reader in the delicate art of exploring the experiences and associations of each individual narrator.

V

Ornamentation as a dimension of style was also adapted from John B. Carroll's *Vectors of Prose Style*[7] and was indexed by the following objective measures: long sentences, wide variation in sentence length, a high proportion of common nouns which are preceded by adjectival or participial modifiers (or a low proportion of unmodified common nouns preceded by 'the'), a high proportion of nouns with Latin suffixes, a low number of verbs denoting physical action, a large number of embedded (dependent) clauses of various types, and a large number of descriptive adjectives (see Table 7 opposite).

Looking down the columns for substantive differences between the narrators, we can make the following observations: the sentences of the Omniscient Narrator, Mr Ramsay, and Lily Briscoe are longer than those of the others, and Mrs McNab's are by far the shortest; the sentences of Mr Ramsay and Lily reveal the greatest variation in sentence lengths, while Mrs McNab's are the most uniform; Charles Tansley and Mrs Ramsay have the lowest percentages of unmodified common nouns, William Bankes and Mr Ramsay have the highest numbers of Latinate nouns; the Omniscient Narrator, Cam,

Table 7

Narrator	Mean Sentence Length (in Syllables)	Standard Deviation of Sentence Lengths	No. Unmodified Common Nouns preceded by 'the'	No. Common Nouns with Latin Suffixes	No. Verbs denoting Physical Action	Per cent Embedded Clauses	No. Descriptive Adjectives
Mrs Ramsay	19·12	17·71	18 14%	10 8%	11 10%	37%	50
Mr Ramsay	30·89	31·59	39 28%	23 17%	11 12%	44%	37
James Ramsay	26·73	24·67	26 20%	9 7%	32 30%	42%	45
Cam Ramsay	26·93	22·29	33 27%	5 4%	34 30%	52%	43
Omniscient	38·27	25·96	52 29%	15 8%	43 40%	47%	49
William Bankes	21·28	21·40	22 17%	29 22%	10 9%	49%	47
Charles Tansley	20·42	24·57	13 11%	4 3%	12 9%	42%	36
Lily Briscoe	32·14	33·74	27 21%	9 7%	15 13%	48%	45
Mrs McNab	15·22	13·22	36 26%	4 3%	15 13%	25%	43

and James have the highest number of 'action' verbs; and Mrs McNab's sentences have the least amount of modification and development.

When we consider all of these items for all of the narrators simultaneously, however, individual differences are immediately greatly depressed; that is, the differences among the narrators tend to cancel out each of the distinguishing linguistic characteristics. Although Mrs Woolf does not differentiate all of the narrators in the same way but characterizes the utterances of some by features which the reader senses over extended passages, the question still remains as to whether each of these items should be considered equally important and therefore be equally weighted. Since they are, all that can be said about the narrators with regard to verbal ornamentation is that the utterances of the Omniscient Narrator, Mr Ramsay, Lily Briscoe, and William Bankes, in that order, are the most adorned; and those of Mrs McNab are the least—with Mrs Ramsay, James, Cam, and Tansley somewhere in between these extremes.

VI

Abstract terms, as used traditionally by rhetoricians, stand for ideas or generalities; more specifically, they tend to describe concepts, qualities, and attitudes which are isolated from their embodiment in a particular, material object. As used in the analysis, then, the term 'abstract noun' will refer to that *noun which has no material thing as a referent.*

Whereas the language of science and philosophy— involving the formulation and elucidation of theoretical argument—tends heavily towards abstraction, the language of literature, of expressive writing, is more apt to be specific and emotive; that is, it tends more towards image and metaphor to achieve its expressive ends. Therefore, the concern here with abstract nouns is *only* for what they might reveal about the mental activity which characterizes the product of each narrator's mind by the way in which he arranges experience conceptually.

Despite the fact that the differentiation between abstract and concrete nouns was primarily determined on the authority of the semanticists, Alfred Korzybski (*Science and Sanity*, Ch. XXV: 'On the Structural Differential') and S. I. Hayakawa, (*Language in Thought and Action*, Ch. X: 'Abstraction Ladder') and despite the sharply circumscribed definition given above, difficulties in differentiating between abstract and concrete nouns are legion. One problem arises with words such as 'gift' and 'figure', words having both abstract and concrete constituents; or when an abstract word such as 'soul' is used concretely to mean a person; or when 'demons', 'angels', 'creatures' are used—words not only of doubtful reference, but also here referring specifically to the Ramsay children. The question arises: Which way should these nouns be counted?

Perhaps the most troublesome aspect results from Mrs Woolf's heavily relying upon concrete words to bear abstract concepts. For example, we find such locutions as: 'the pulp had gone out of their friendship' — 'pulp' meaning the solidarity of the relationship; or 'their paths lying different ways' — with 'paths' referring to careers, interests, ways of life, and so on. These nouns and many similar ones were considered abstract and were counted as such.

It seems necessary to stress, therefore, that although another stylistician with the same samples might consider more, less, or even different nouns to be abstract, these counts are nevertheless fairly reliable. For in spite of these difficulties in deciding which way to count certain of them, by using so restrictive a definition of abstract noun, at least consistency was possible from one choice to the next and from one sample to the next; and that consistency, in turn, made possible a quite accurate index of the *relative differences* among the various narrators. These

Table 8

Narrator	Abstract Nouns (including Gerunds)
Mrs Ramsay	50
Mr Ramsay	72
James Ramsay	24
Cam Ramsay	16
Omniscient	36
William Bankes	74
Charles Tansley	30
Lily Briscoe	45
Mrs McNab	19

quantities vigorously reinforce the critical judgments made in Chapter Five with regard to each narrator's individual characteristics and his tendency to conceptualize experience.

Although the number of abstract nouns in Mrs Ramsay's sample may seem high for someone preoccupied with immediate material surroundings and not particularly given to intellectual cerebration, she is nevertheless an individual whose thoughts gravitate towards her love for her children, her self-sacrifice, her isolation in a hostile world, her marriage; and these, of course, are not materially-bound categories which can be thought of in concrete terms.

If the language of intellectual activity is necessarily the language of abstraction, then the extent to which Mr Ramsay uses abstract nouns is self-evident. One can not ponder on 'fame', 'genius', 'death', 'wastes of the ages', 'human ignorance', et cetera, as does this philosopher, without becoming highly abstract. Thus, for a man of his intellectual calibre, a high proportion of abstract nouns is not only appropriate, but also expected.

Conversely, the low proportion of abstract nouns in the samples of James and Cam is consistent with their youth. For just as abstract words filter into a language, to any significant degree, only relatively late in its development, so too, abstract words enter an individual's vocabulary and become part of his usage only when he is mature enough and sufficiently educated to arrange the ingredients of his experiential life along conceptual lines; that is, when he is capable of sensing patterns and making generalizations.

Similarly, Mrs McNab, although mature enough, because she lacks the education and the intellectual training that take one beyond the realm of earth-bound objects, has very little use for verbal symbols which do not point to material things.

That the number of abstract nouns in the Omniscient Narrator's utterances should be as low as it is, is not surprising when we consider the poetic prose section from which the sample was extracted. In expressive writing, the language—being more emotive—tends to be more concrete, more specific; it is apt to rely more on image and metaphor to achieve its aesthetic ends. That relatively few abstract nouns should be found in the sample, therefore, is consistent with the lyrical method Mrs Woolf employs to conjure up the sense of the destructive whirlwinds of time and nature's indifference to human effort. The language only really becomes abstract in the brief mystical passage concerned with 'divine goodness' and 'human penitence'.

William Bankes' sample contains the highest number of abstract nouns. It supports convincingly the statement that while the language of expressive writing is concrete, the language of science and philosophy is more abstract; and while the sample is not written in scientific language, Mr Bankes, himself a scientist—a botanist—relies considerably upon abstract words to formulate his thoughts. Secondly, we have only to consider such phrases as 'his natural *air*', 'their *paths* lying different *ways*', 'get into a *groove*', to realize that in his sample, more than any other, nouns (those italicized), ordinarily concrete, are used in an abstract sense. As with Mr Ramsay, Bankes' dominant abstract nouns—'friendship', 'fault', 'interruptions', 'affection', 'waste of time', 'questions', 'life', for example—not only bespeak the concerns of an educated and highly civilized mind, but also they illuminate the intricate cross-currents of an isolated man's solitary, experiential life.

Charles Tansley's abstract nouns indicate a relatively aggressive and immature individual whose interests are, for the most part, competitive and materially-oriented. That he uses so few is due to the fact that it is difficult to be so angry and frustrated as he is and abstract at the same time. Anger, if it is to be relieved, must necessarily be directed at objects of the material world. And so it is: such words as 'rot' (meaning useless social intercourse, as he uses it), 'nonsense', 'lies', 'silliness', 'debt' are all abstract nouns which are directly connected with earth-bound categories of people and things—objects on which Tansley must vent his spleen.

In so far as Lily Briscoe's use of abstract nouns is concerned, it would be tempting to say that, because the quantity is slightly above the mean value (40·7), she represents that duality of personality in which the intellectual, sensitive part abstracts experience, while the artistic, intuitive moiety senses life as concrete, specific, on the 'level of ordinary experience'. Like Mr Bankes', many of her nouns are concrete, but they are used in an abstract sense. For example, when she speaks of the 'golden mesh', she is referring to Mrs Ramsay's mysteriousness; when she says 'whatever laurels', figuratively, she means honours, recognition; when she refers to her 'painting', in a sense, she is speaking of her ambition, her aspirations.

Approximately two-thirds of her abstract nouns, directly or indirectly, have to do with Mrs Ramsay; and among them are encountered those of the highest level of abstraction. This is an extremely significant percentage when we realize that Lily must ultimately abstract Mrs Ramsay entirely before she is able, finally—as the artist —to see the integration, the conceptual arrangement and harmony her painting requires, something which is not possible while Mrs Ramsay's corporeal presence intrudes itself as a material influence on her artistic sensibility.

VII

The term 'image', used in this analysis, refers to that evocative linguistic construct which helps to define the mood, tone, and meaning of the pasasge in which it occurs. An image makes its appeal through the senses and invites the reconstruction of a sense experience drawn from the reader's personal history; that is, an image appeals to a reader's originally sensory impressions, causing him to experience—*beyond* the printed page— something residual in himself.

The images in each of the samples were examined for what they revealed about the personality and character of the narrator using them. In a sense, the analysis is similar to Caroline Spurgeon's demonstration, for example, of how Shakespeare, through images, indicated the change that took place in Falstaff's character between Part I and Part II of *Henry IV*.[8] And if, as I. A. Richards wrote, 'What gives an image efficacy is . . . its character as a mental event peculiarly connected with sensation',[9] then this segment of the analysis, in addition to suggesting the quality of the narrator's emotional and intellectual life, tells us something of his relationship to experience. Moreover, we discover not only how images function evaluatively to reveal the attitude of the narrator, but also how that attitude works rhetorically to control and shape the reader's responses.[10] And finally, we will see how, for Mrs Woolf, imagery becomes a technical device by which she differentiates one narrator from another.

In Mrs Ramsay

1 demons of wickedness (18)*
2 angels of delight (18)
3 never to see them grow up into long-legged monsters (18)
4 Prue, a perfect angel (23)
5 they were both wild creatures (25)
6 in they came, fresh as roses (40)
7 found them netted in their cots like birds among cherries and raspberries (40)
8 making up stories about some little bit of rubbish— something they had heard (40)
9 They had all their little treasures (41)
10 a little strip of time presented itself to her eyes—her fifty years (51)
11 she called life terrible, hostile, and quick to pounce on you if you gave it a chance (53)

* The number preceding the image enumerates it consecutively and appears in the discussions in parentheses to make the reference clear. The number in parentheses following each image refers to the sentence in which it occurs (see Appendix A). I have used this notation consistently throughout.

The first nine (82%) of the eleven images are characteristically devoted to children. Whether she refers to them as 'demons of wickedness' (1) or 'wild creatures' (5), her tone indicates that she feels great tenderness for them and that for her, all children are essentially 'angels of delight' (2). It is only when we learn that she never wants 'to see them grow up into long legged monsters' (3) that we might begin to suspect her relations with adults and with the adult world: why she calls life 'terrible, hostile, and quick to pounce on you if you gave it a chance' (11). Fragile though this connection may seem, it bears the kernel idea of Mrs Ramsay's orientation to life and to people; and, as a reading of the entire novel reveals, it is an eloquent, though elliptical, pronouncement of the basic reason she feels so acutely the inadequacy of adult human relations.

In Mr Ramsay

1 the geranium . . . displayed among its leaves . . . that obvious distinction between the two classes of men (1)
2 the steady goers of superhuman strength (1)
3 the inspired who, miraculously, lump all the letters together in one flash (1)
4 feelings that would not have disgraced a leader . . . stole upon him (5)
5 trying to the end to pierce the darkness (6)
6 the leader of a forlorn hope (10)
7 if you looked from a mountain top down the long wastes of the ages (17)
8 His own little light would shine . . . and would be merged in some bigger light, and that in a bigger still (19)
9 high enough to see the waste of the years and the perishing of stars (20)
10 if before death stiffens his limbs (20)
11 cairns raised by grateful followers over his bones (21)
12 used his strength wholly to the last ounce (22)
13 the hero puts his armour off [Mr Ramsay] (24)

14 in intensity of his isolation and the waste of ages and the perishing of the stars (24)

15 he does homage to the beauty of the world [Mrs Ramsay] (24)

16 the sight of human ignorance and human fate (26)

17 the sea eating the ground (26)

18 the sternness at the heart of her beauty (29)

Tracing even the manifest content of the eighteen images isolated in his sample, we see more forcefully, though less comprehensively, the emotional organization which characterizes Mr Ramsay's experience of living. Note, for example, how closely related and overlapping for him are his work, his philosophical interests, his sense of intellectual inadequacy, the brevity of fame in the length of posterity. Intermingled with these images of disunity and isolation are the highly affective associations of 'the leader of a forlorn hope' (6) who will persevere to the end, who will use 'his strength wholly to the last ounce (12) . . . before death stiffens his limbs' (10).

As his fantasies of perishing stars and 'the waste of ages' (14) and 'human ignorance' (16) multiply and enlarge, we feel not so much the 'intensity of his isolation' (14) or the gloom generated by his thoughts, as we are quickened to the nobility and courage of a man who, although alive to the buffets in human destiny, wants still to do 'homage to the beauty of the world' (15), wants still to remain immersed in the human concourse which his wife and children constitute.

In James Ramsay

1 I shall take a knife and strike him to the heart (3)

2 but it was the thing that descended on him (4)

3 that fierce sudden black-winged harpy, with its talons and its beak all cold and hard, that struck and struck at you (4)

4 he could feel the beak on his bare legs, where it had struck when he was a child (4)

143

5 that he would kill, that he would strike to the heart (5)
6 that he would track down and stamp out—tyranny, despotism (6)
7 cutting off their right to speak (6)
8 the black wings spread (10)
9 the hard beak tore (10)
10 pressing a sovereign into some frozen old woman's hand (13)
11 at the head of the table dead silent (14)
12 there was a waste of snow and rock very lonely and austere (15)
13 there were two pairs of footprints only; his own and his father's (15)
14 Suppose . . . he had seen a waggon crush ignorantly and innocently, some one's foot (18)
15 Suppose he had seen the foot first, in the grass, smooth, and whole (19)
16 then the wheel; and the same foot, purple, crushed (19)
17 But the wheel was innocent (20)
18 down it came over his foot, over Cam's foot, over anybody's foot (21)
19 the blinds were sucked in and out by the breeze (28)
20 and over all those plates and bowls and tall brandishing red and yellow flowers a very thin yellow veil would be drawn, like a vine leaf, at night (28)
21 But the leaf-like veil was so fine (30)
22 lights lifted it (30)
23 voices crinkled it (30)
24 some dress rustling (30)
25 some chain tinkling (30)
26 It was in this world that the wheel went over the person's foot (31)
27 Something, he remembered, stayed and darkened over him; would not move (32)
28 something flourished up in the air (32)
29 something arid and sharp descended even there, like a blade, a scimitar, smiting through the leaves and flowers

even of that happy world and making it shrivel and fall (32)

30 The Lighthouse was then a silvery, misty-looking tower with a yellow eye, that opened suddenly, and softly in the evening (34)

The rush of imagery in James' sample accords with the character sketch of him made in the critical reading of the novel because they point up his dominant preoccupations. Among them are the rivalry and jealousy he feels towards his father, expressed in terms of violence and death (1, 5, 6). Equally significant, and possibly justifying James' wish to strike his father dead, are the nine images (2, 3, 4, 7, 8, 9, 27, 28, 29) which reveal the ways he sees him: either as 'that fierce sudden black-winged harpy, with its talons and its beak all cold and hard, that struck and struck at you' (3) or as 'something arid and sharp [that] descended even there, like a blade, a scimitar . . .' (29). The images of his father and those of his death occupy forty per cent of the total number.

Closely associated with them and curiously reflecting a different attitude towards his father are the six images of the wagon wheel figuratively crushing someone's foot (14, 15, 16, 17, 18, 26). The images occur while James is searching his memory for the cause of the hatred and terror he feels for his father. And while he sees his father's representing that destructive wagon, he thinks: 'But the wheel was innocent' (17). It is precisely because James is unaware that the wheel refers to his father and unaware that he does not hate his father so much as he wishes to be accepted by him, to identify with him, that the imagery assumes a peculiar kind of rhetorical significance; by that I mean, the reader becomes an active participant in James' unconscious change of feeling, because he is able to make connections with and see implications in that change which James, himself, is wholly unaware of. That unconscious wish to identify with his father, for example, is located in the image which significantly introduces the wheel-foot passage: 'there were two pairs of footprints only; his own and his father's' (13).

If we recall that James, at the age of six, saw his mother as the 'rosy-flowered fruit tree laid with leaves', we discover that now, at sixteen, while he is searching through his palimpsest of memory, trying to recreate that world in which the wheel crushed the foot, his mother very subtly emerges in the imagery: first, as the 'very thin yellow veil [that] would be drawn, like a vine leaf, at night' (20); and then connects with the following: 'the leaf-like veil was so fine' (21), 'lights lifted it' (22), 'voices crinkled it' (23); until finally the arid blade, the scimitar descends, 'smiting through the leaves and flowers . . . making it shrivel and fall' (29).

The imagery in this passage is technically brilliant because beyond its overt statement, it functions to uncover the more profound meaning of the relationship between mother and father and son. Because the veil is 'leaf-like' —a 'vine leaf'—it strongly suggests a connection with the intricate entanglement of the hedge which grew to symbolize the emotional barrier separating husband and wife; but more than that, the 'life-like veil' suggests the same living thing symbolically veiling—separating— father from son.

Equally brilliant is James' image of his father as 'a waste of snow and rock very lonely and austere' (12), because it functions simultaneously in three ways. First, it connects with and reinforces Mr Ramsay's image of himself as the 'leader of a forlorn hope' in the snow on some mountain top, looking for a crag of rock. Second, it indicates the empathy of son for father as well as the extent to which he has already unconsciously identified with his father's thoughts of himself. Third, the words, 'very lonely and austere', reveal the deep, though unuttered, understanding and compassion James feels for Mr Ramsay. But what is most remarkable about all of this imagery is that although he is unaware of many of his latent feelings, James' images reveal those feelings and, at the same time, subtly prepare the reader for the final reconciliation between father and son. It does this while simultaneously linking together widely separated sections of the novel.

In Cam Ramsay

1 the sea swept in (2)
2 [the island] . . . shaped something like a leaf stood on end (3)
3 all had slipped, all had passed, all had streamed away (5)
4 shaped something like a leaf stood on its end (8)
5 the gold-sprinkled waters flowing (8)
6 they were crackling in front of them the pages (12)
7 Then they took all this with their clean hands [Cam's questions] (13)
8 and they brushed the scraps together (13)
9 one could let whatever one thought expand here like a leaf in water (15)
10 and *The Times* crackling (15)
11 the shiny cover mottled like a plover's egg (18)
12 He is a sarcastic brute [James about his father] (21)
13 his legs curled (27)
14 He read, she thought, as if he were guiding something (30)
15 or wheedling a large flock of sheep (30)
16 or pushing his way up and up a single narrow path (30)
17 and sometimes he went fast and straight, and broke his way through the bramble (30)
18 and sometimes it seemed a branch struck at him (30)
19 a bramble blinded him (30)
20 on he went, tossing over page after page (30)
21 But the leaf was losing its sharpness (33)
22 but then like a bird, he spread his wings (39)
23 he floated off to settle out of your reach somewhere far away on some desolate stump (39)

Most of the twenty-three images of Cam's sample function to buffer the harshness of James' outward attitude towards his father. The first five, for example, not only create a mood of serenity but also prepare the reader for the happy memories that filter through Cam's mind as she recalls the security of her father's study, where the old gentlemen sat with newspapers, answering her youthful questions. As we become increasingly persuaded to share her feelings towards her father, there appears the image of his book's 'shiny cover mottled like a plover's egg' (11). The image works in a very important way: since we associate Mr Ramsay with books, most readers will readily, though perhaps unconsciously, link up with him their affective associations of the soft-tipped bill of the plover—significantly different from James' image of the 'black-winged harpy, with . . . its beak all cold and hard, that struck and struck'.

Her sympathetic view of her father enlarges when she compares his reading to 'guiding something or wheedling a large flock of sheep' (14, 15). This analogy, too, is important because indirectly his reading and his book become equated with his intellect; and in that, she sees him not only as an intellectual leader guiding flocks of less knowledgeable men, but also as a man who perseveres through numerous obstacles, through numerous philosophical 'brambles' (17, 18, 19, 20) which strike and blind him.

Cam also senses in him an intense isolation; but for her, he is not the harpy that descends on one, as he is for James; rather, he is that bird which spreads it wings (22) and 'floated off to settle out of your reach somewhere far away on some desolate stump' (23). This important image works in two ways: first, it counters the rapacity expressed in James' bird imagery; and second, it reinforces the idea of Mr Ramsay's loneliness and isolation—and indeed his gentleness—by the rhetorical function of the words 'floated', 'settle', 'far away', 'desolate stump'.

In the Omniscient Narrator

1 the moon sunk (1)
2 a thin rain drumming on the roof (1)

3 a downpouring of immense darkness began (1)

4 nothing . . . could survive the flood (2)

5 the profusion of darkness which, creeping in at keyholes and crevices (2)

6 stole round window blinds (2)

7 came into bedrooms (2)

8 swallowed up here a jug and basin (2)

9 Not only was furniture confounded (3)

10 Sometimes a hand was raised as if to clutch something or ward something off (4)

11 or somebody groaned, or somebody laughed aloud as if sharing a joke with nothingness (4)

12 Only through the rusty hinges and swollen sea-moistened woodwork (6)

13 certain airs, detached from the body of the wind . . . crept round corners and ventured indoors (6)

14 they entered the drawing-room questioning and wondering (7)

15 toying with the flap of hanging wall-paper (7)

16 asking, would it hang much longer, when would it fall (7)

17 Then smoothly brushing the walls, they passed on musingly as if asking the red and yellow roses on the wall-paper whether they would fade (8)

18 and questioning . . . the torn letters in the waste-paper basket, the flowers, the books . . . asking, Were they allies? Were they enemies? How long would they endure? (8)

19 some random light directing them with its pale footfall upon stair and mat, from some uncovered star, or wandering ship, or the Lighthouse even (9)

20 the little airs mounted the staircase (9)

21 and nosed round bedroom doors (9)

22 Here one might say to those sliding lights (12)

23 those fumbling airs that breathe and bend over the bed itself (12)

24 Upon which, wearily, ghostlily, as if they had feather-light fingers and the light persistency of feathers, they

would look once on the shut eyes, and the loosely clasping fingers (13)

25 and fold their garments wearily and disappear (13)

26 And so nosing, rubbing, they went to the window on the staircase, to the servants' bedrooms, to the boxes in the attics (14)

27 descending, blanched the apples on the dining-room table (14)

28 fumbled the petals of roses (14)

29 tried the picture on the easel (14)

30 brushed the mat (14)

31 and blew a little sand along the floor (14)

32 At length, desisting, all ceased together (15)

33 gathered together (15)

34 all sighed together (15)

35 all together gave off an aimless gust of lamentation (15)

36 to which some door in the kitchen replied; swung wide; admitted nothing; and slammed to (15)

37 A short space, especially when the darkness dims so soon (19)

38 a faint green quickens, like a turning leaf, in the hollow of the wave (19)

39 The winter holds a pack of them in store [nights] (21)

40 and deals them equally, evenly, with indefatigable fingers (21)

41 Some of them hold aloft clear planets, plates of brightness (23)

42 The autumn trees, ravaged as they are, take on the flash of tattered flags kindling in the gloom of cool cathedral caves (24)

43 where gold letters on marble pages describe death in battle and how bones bleach and burn far away in Indian sands (24)

44 in the light of harvest moons, the light which mellows the energy of labour (25)

45 and smooths the stubble (25)

46 and brings the wave lapping blue to the shore (25)

47 touched by human penitence and all its toil, divine

     goodness had parted the curtain and displayed behind
     it, single, distinct, the hare erect; the wave falling; the
     boat rocking (26)
48 divine goodness, twitching the cord, draws the curtain;
     it does not please him (26)
49 he covers his treasures in a drench of hail, and so breaks
     them, so confuses them that it seems impossible that
     their calm should ever return (27)
50 or that we should ever compose from their fragments a
     perfect whole (27)
51 or read in the littered pieces the clear words of truth (27)
52 For our penitence deserves a glimpse only; our toil
     respite only (28)
53 The nights now are full of wind and destruction (29)
54 the trees plunge and bend (29)
55 and their leaves fly helter skelter until the lawn is
     plastered with them (29)
56 and choke rain pipes (29)
57 and scatter damp paths (29)
58 Also the sea tosses itself and breaks itself (30)

In this image-freighted sample is some of Virginia
Woolf's most hauntingly poetic writing. Dramatized for us
are the procession of nights, the pageant of seasons, the
passing of years. The two most salient features of the
imagery as a whole are its expansion from the particular
to the general and its progression from restlessness to
turbulence.

Of the fifty-eight images listed, the first nine introduce
and personify night—a particular, unspecified night—
'creeping in at keyholes and crevices' (5) furtively searching and meeting unnamed presences (10, 11) of the past,
lurking throughout the house. In the twenty-three which
follow (13-35) come the 'certain airs' (13), directed by
'some random light' (19) which 'crept round corners and
ventured indoors' questioning, hovering over the rem-
nants of decay, the pillories of time. And from the solitude
of the spoiled house, the next ten images (36-46) turn

to the generalized nights outside which winter deals out 'with indefatigable fingers' (40), nights which hold 'aloft clear planets' (41), kindling ravaged 'autumn trees' (42).

In the six images which follow (47-52), human life and nature's indifference become surrounded by a mystical aura from which subtly emanates a tonally depressed complex of ideas associated with human penitence, divine goodness, fragments of truth, human loss.

With an abrupt change in mood and cadence, nights are introduced again, now 'full of wind and destruction' (53), now with all their immediacy and urgency, causing trees to 'plunge and bend' (54), leaves to 'fly helter skelter' (55) choking rain pipes and scattering damp paths (56, 57); and with no alteration of pitch, the sea, too, tossing and breaking itself (58), is brought to life in all its recklessness and flux and violence.

In this remarkable section, through images alone and the countless associations they evoke, Virginia Woolf not only contrasts the idea of human time with nature's timelessness, but also points up its capriciousness and indifference to man's transitory stay on earth. And by animating the fumbling airs, the random light, the destructive nights, she dramatizes the forces of nature to the extent that life and death, human creation and natural disintegration, become intermingled with rhythmic emotional fibres giving the whole section an organic integrity, which simultaneously prepares us for—indeed, propels us towards—the final movement of the novel.

In William Bankes

1 hung round with that solitude [Mr Ramsay] (5)
2 the pulp had gone out of their friendship (8)
3 but there, like the body of a young man laid up in peat for a century, with the red fresh on his lips, was his friendship (11)
4 laid up across the bay (11)

5 he was anxious . . . to clear himself in his own mind from the imputation of having dried and shrunk (12)
6 their paths lying different ways (13)
7 People soon drift apart (14)
8 He had not drifted apart (15)
9 he never let himself get into a groove (16)
10 He had friends in all circles (17)
11 friendships, even the best of them, are frail things (44)
12 One drifts apart (45)

Scarce though they are, the images here are consonant with the character of Bankes described in the critical analysis of the novel. One of the outstanding features of these images is that all of them, with two exceptions (1, 5), are manifestly concerned, in one way or another, with friendships. What is not obvious in the sample, but what is pointed up by the images themselves, is the negativity revealed in their latent content: that is, his idea of friendship is surrounded by words which have a tendency to negate whatever appeal meaningful human ties may have for a man like Bankes. Consider the following, for example: 'like the body of a young man laid up in peat for a century . . . was his friendship' (3) or 'the pulp had gone out of their friendship' (2) or 'People soon drift apart' (7) or 'One drifts apart' (12) or 'friendships . . . are frail things' (11).

His most revealing utterance indicates the anxiety he harbours in wishing to clear himself (with regard to his friendship with Mr Ramsay) from 'the imputation of having dried and shrunk' (5). The statement is a rationalization of a man who indeed has 'friends in all circles' (10), who 'never let[s] himself get into a groove' (9). The reason for having friends in all circles, without having firmly-established friendships, originates in his need to keep a great emotional distance between himself and others, because his wells of feeling have frozen hard; and in all probability, as a social being, he has 'dried and shrunk'.

VIRGINIA WOOLF'S LIGHTHOUSE
In Charles Tansley

1 With stars in her eyes (13)
2 and veils in her hair (13)
3 with cyclamen and wild violets (13)
4 Stepping through fields of flowers and taking to her breast buds that had broken and lambs that had fallen (15)
5 with the stars in her eyes (15)
6 and the wind in her hair (15)
7 the sort of rot these people wanted him to talk (17)
8 it all seemed to him silly, superficial, flimsy (19)
9 They did nothing but talk, talk, talk, eat, eat, eat (27)
10 He felt very rough (37)
11 not going to be made a fool of (39)
12 he had never run a penny into debt (44)
13 he wished it had not come out all in a jerk like that (45)
14 he was not just a dry prig (47)
15 Ramsay had dished himself (53)

What is most conspicuous in Tansley's images is his tendency towards exaggeration. The first six, for example, indicate not only that he is quite carried away with the beauty of the fifty-year-old Mrs Ramsay, but also that his feelings transport him to absurd extremes.

In the next three images (7, 8, 9), the words 'rot', 'silly, superficial, flimsy', and 'did nothing but talk, talk, talk, eat, eat, eat' also clearly point up the vindictiveness which permeates his personality and which expresses itself with singular force when he feels—or rather thinks he is being made to feel—'very rough' (10) or that he is being 'made a fool of' (11). Of particular interest is the glaring and peculiar admixture of self-defence and self-depreciation he expresses through such self-reflections as 'all in a jerk' (13) and 'not just a dry prig' (14).

But it is especially important to notice that when his sense of unworthiness overpowers his precarious self-esteem, in order to squelch immediately the misery of that feeling, he savagely disparages his host—who 'had dished himself' (15)—and, by extension, everyone else present.

Consistent with the personality deduced earlier (Chapter Five), the images isolated in his sample reflect in very concentrated form the smouldering resentment which characterizes Tansley and which has its source in his sense of inferiority, alienation, and neurotic pride.

In Lily Briscoe

1 the shapes etherealized (5)
2 the colour burning on a framework of steel (7)
3 the light of a butterfly's wing lying upon the arches of a cathedral (7)
4 a few random marks scrawled upon the canvas remained (8)
5 She had been annoyed . . . by some highhandedness (12)
6 they could seek shelter under the shade which Mr Bankes extended over them both (13)
7 which seemed to her like clods with no life in them [her paint mounds] (15)
8 she would inspire them (15)
9 force them to move (15)
10 flow (15)
11 do her bidding tomorrow (15)
12 had you found a crumpled glove in the corner of the sofa, you would have known it, from its twisted finger, hers indisputably (17)
13 she was like a bird for speed (18)
14 an arrow for directness (18)
15 Mr Carmichael snuffling and sniffling (22)
16 All this she would adroitly shape; even maliciously twist [Mrs Ramsay] (23)
17 whatever laurels might be tossed to her (23)
18 all this seemed so little, so virginal (26)
19 and white lights parted the curtains (27)
20 and even now and then some bird chirped in the garden (27)

21 a serious stare from eyes of unparalleled depth (27)

22 confront Mrs Ramsay's simple certainty (27)

23 her little Brisk was a fool (27)

24 Mrs Ramsay presiding with immutable calm over destinies she completely failed to understand (28)

25 this was the glove's twisted finger (30)

26 But into what sanctuary had one penetrated (31)

27 and in its stead, something clear as the space which the clouds at last uncover [Mrs Ramsay's wilfulness gone] (32)

28 the little space of sky which sleeps beside the moon (32)

29 one's perceptions . . . were tangled in a golden mesh (35)

30 did she lock up within her some secret (35)

31 Every one could not be as helter skelter, hand to mouth as she was [Mrs Ramsay] (36)

Of the thirty-one images listed here, nine (1–4, 7–11) have to do with Lily's painting and two (17, 18) with her status and future as a painter. Twenty images (65%), in one way or another, have to do with Mrs Ramsay: how she seemed to Lily (5, 12, 13, 14, 21, 22, 24, 25, 29, 31); what Mrs Ramsay said (15, 23) or how she said it (16); Lily's attempt to probe her mysteriousness (26, 27, 30); the past when both of them talked through the night; and Bankes' feeling towards Mrs Ramsay (6).

There are two significant points to be made about Lily's images. First, those concerned with Mrs Ramsay express a great deal of ambivalence. For example, the image of the glove's twisted finger (12), by the very associations it calls forth, suggests something negative, sinister, about Mrs Ramsay; and we discover what it is when Lily thinks that 'All this she would adroitly shape; even *maliciously twist*' (16).[11] Secondly, the subtle and complex insinuations in her imagery suggest that of all the *personae*, Lily is the most acutely aware of the multiplicity of shapes a human being is capable of assuming, of the enigmatic shadows which proliferate in the impenetrable depth of people, making one's perception of them imperfect, opaque, deceptive. It is because of this sensibility that Lily, as artist, is privileged finally to create harmony out of the chaos—to know, also, that her vision of life and human beings will have constantly to be renewed, constantly to be made over.

In Mrs McNab

1 without a soul in it [the house] (5)
2 all run to riot [the garden] (19)
3 Fiery, like all red-haired women (38)
4 Whatever did they want to hang a beast's skull there? gone mouldy too (46)
5 the old gentleman, lean as a rake, wagging his head [Mr Ramsay] (53)

The dearth of images found in Mrs McNab's sample is as indicative as the abundance found in some of the others. As an uneducated, practical utilitarian, concerned with the concrete 'here and now', Mrs McNab is not given to image-creation, to the precision of metaphoric language. It is interesting, however, to see how, with only five images, Virginia Woolf so skilfully delineates this narrator.

In the first image, not only is the word, 'soul', referring to a person, a threadbare cliché, but also it is consistent with the vocabulary of an Irish Catholic charwoman. The same applies to 'fiery', which refers to quick-tempered, explosive 'red-haired women' (3): not only is the chromatic and thermal connection a simple one, but so too is the association with the stereotype of the irascible Irish cook.

The garden's condition, 'all run to riot' (2) and Mr Ramsay's being 'as lean as a rake' (5) have also obvious connections to each other is so far as gardening is concerned. But when we add to these, the skull's being 'mouldy too' (4), we immediately see that Mrs McNab's chief preoccupations are all connected with her work, her cleaning, with keeping order in any domestic setting—whether it means seeing to it that the garden is maintained or scrubbing mould off a neglected and long-forgotten childhood relic.

Chapter Seven

CONCLUSION

A NOVEL can, and often does, present new problems when it offers a set of attitudes which are difficult precisely to determine and even more difficult to explain. The multiple facets of the divided personality, such as that of Hesse's Harry Haller in *Der Steppenwolf*; the gradual moral disintegration of Gide's Michel in *L'Immoraliste*; the philosophical inflections of Jean-Baptiste Clamence's monologue on innocence, judgment, and conscience in Camus' *La Chute*; the conflicts and confusions of sexual identity in Djuna Barnes' *Nightwood*; the perceptions and visions of Mathias, the homicidal maniac in Robbe-Grillet's *Le Voyeur*; the ethical implications of violence and despair in Céline's *Voyage au bout de la nuit*; Barabbas' tortured stretch between the world of reality and the world of faith in Lagerkvist's novel of that name—all of these, to mention but a few, are moral issues and values as difficult to communicate as they are to understand in all their complexity and subtlety.

When we consider the complex dynamics of the literary experience itself,[1] the numerous devices for achieving literary effects, the intricate and countless factors involved in the transaction between reader and text, it is not surprising to discover how many novels—multiple-point-of-view or not—are misread and how many readers are incapable of responding appropriately to what is before them on the printed page. The principal reason, I think, is that too few readers pay enough attention to the *persona*, to the voice narrating the story.

Unless we are aware of the angle of narration from which the utterances are being made, we will be unable to examine critically the content of what is said; we will be unable to evaluate the significance of the sequence of what is said; and, most important, we will be unable to determine the reliability of the narrator saying it. When such narrator-awareness is lacking, it is not uncommon to find someone judging, for example, Barabbas, a stubborn and insensitive atheist, rather than seeing him as that tragically isolated non-believer in a frenzied world of blind faith; or seeing James' governess as a self-sacrificing and heroic mistress rather than as a sexually-obsessed neurotic.

This kind of misreading does not only happen with the general reader: unfortunately, critics, too, who dedicate their efforts to myth-mongering, symbol-hunting, type-categorizing, and the like—too preoccupied to attend to something so basic as point of view—have produced texts which reverberate with critical distortion and confusion.

Theoretically and actually, the multiple-point-of-view novel is *sui generis* not specifically because multiple narrators are involved, but rather because the mode of narration is of necessity, impersonal; and by that I mean, the novelist must deal with the technical problem of somehow informing the reader that he is presenting values and beliefs through his various narrators which he, himself, may or may not always share. In other words, when multiple angles of narration are employed, the author nowhere allows himself the privilege of explicit evaluative commentary. Instead, the reader himself must, by a series of movements from and adjustments to one narrator after another, piece the story together, evaluate the fictional material presented to him, sense the sequence of narrators and narrative progress, and, finally, make of the total something meaningful. This, by itself, requires considerable effort on a reader's part; and even more effort—not to mention an increased frustration tolerance—is required when the narrators are not readily identifiable.

For this reason Virginia Woolf's *To the Lighthouse*

serves as a model for developing a systematic critical approach to the multiple-point-of-view novel. Because of its level of complexity and difficulty, many of the subtlest problems of technique and methods of criticism could be dealt with which might not otherwise have been possible had a less comprehensive work been selected.

In tracing the technical evolution of point of view from omniscient narration to direct mental transmission (i.e., impersonal narration), considerable care was taken not only to point out how a novelist, by using this or that angle of narration, achieved certain literary effects, but also to indicate how the reader was affected; that is, how point of view, as technique, functioned rhetorically to elicit certain responses from the reader—responses necessary for the appropriate organization of the text.

Since in the multiple-point-of-view novel, the sequence of events which orders the reader's view of the fictional world is essentially equivalent to the sequence of narrators, the method of analysis developed in this study does away with that artificial distinction between form and content. For just as the novel's form depends on the proportion and duration of the events which constitute content, so too does content depend upon a particular sequence of presentation if its meaning is to come across effectively. Thus I have tried to stress that if we attend to the proportion allotted some events as against others, the length of time they are allowed in the total work, the consciousness through which the material is being filtered, and the sequence of the narrations, we are essentially examining what the author has chosen, out of all that is available to him, to communicate his meaning. And in those choices is located the rhetoric which realizes the work's aesthetic centre and semantic design; for through those choices, only, has the subjective novelist—the 'silent' author—been able unobtrusively to comment and implicitly to pass judgments which guide us through his fictional world of real values—values established for us to share and respond to appropriately.

The question of appropriate response to a novel is a pivotal one. If we think back on our experiences with such earlier novels as Dickens' *Hard Times*, George Eliot's *Middlemarch*, Reade's *The Cloister and the Hearth*, Scott's *The Heart of Midlothian*, Meredith's *The Egoist*, Emily Brontë's *Wuthering Heights* and consider such strategic structural elements as the chronological ordering of action or such stylistic conventions as the use of explicity didactic normative words or morally-charged honorific locutions[2] or the frequent appearance of the vocative case—the 'Dear Reader' variety—or the little sermon-like digressions generously distributed throughout the text, we realize that, despite the diversity of external detail, there is implicitly assumed a cultural stability, an established and honoured moral code—a view of reality held in common. It is only in this kind of emotional and philosophical climate that an Anthony Trollope in his *Doctor Thorne*, for example, may write:

> It can hardly be expected that any one will consent to go through with a fiction that offers so little of allurement in its first pages; but twist it as I will I cannot do otherwise. I find that I cannot make poor Mr Gresham hem and haw and turn himself uneasily in his arm-chair in a natural manner till I have said why he is uneasy. I cannot bring in my doctor speaking his mind freely among the bigwigs till I have explained that it is in accordance with his usual character to do so. This is unartistic on my part, and shows want of imagination as well as want of skill.

or may conclude *Barchester Towers* with:

> The Author now leaves him in the hands of his readers; not as a hero, not as a man to be admired and talked of, not as a man who should be toasted at public dinners and spoken of with conventional absurdity as a perfect divine, but as a good man without guile, believing humbly in the religion which he has striven to teach, and guided by the precepts which he has striven to learn.

CONCLUSION

Quiescent in such a culture is the urge for introspection or the quest for identity, because the limits of reality are clearly defined as is the individual's relationship to it. When such circumstances prevail, it seems unlikely that a reader will bring to the text awarenesses alien to the emotional alignments and ethical preoccupations of his society and time. In other words, both author and reader are in a kind of tacit agreement as to what should or should not be.

But when reality becomes questionable, meretricious, when life becomes the dumb-show mocking the stark actualities of experience, then the very foundations of the social structure begin to quake. With it dissolve many of the shared values necessary for cultural cohesion. It is then that the individual mind turns inwards in its search for coherence, for some orderly scheme from which the individual's inherited beliefs and moral sanctions may derive validation and meaning.

In these circumstances, the author can no longer assume the privilege of entering into and overtly criticizing or commenting on the fictional people and events. He can not because socially determined points of reference are obscured, and the reader is no longer in unequivocal agreement with the author: now, both have values and standards which are at least highly personal and at most highly inflexible. And it is in such times of cultural debacle—when values are tentative and omniscient narration becomes a paradox—that the author withdraws from his novel and relegates to narrators the task of persuading the reader to his system of values.

It is not only suitable, then, but also logical, in an age of such ethical diversity and relativism, that the manifold-consciousness method should have emerged and marked the highest point of development in the novel's evolution. While the method of impersonal narration requires almost complete auctorial reticence, the current idea of 'Exit author, exit reader' could not be further from the truth. In fact, the opposite is more nearly true: Exit author;

163

enter reader. Perhaps more than any other, the multiple-point-of-view novel, with its author abdicating his position as ultimate authority, requires of the reader constant and creative participation. Also, because of its design of numerous subjective impressions, it offers the reader one of the most authentic contemporary records of human and moral values as well as the most singularly accurate sense of what reality means to the twentieth-century mind.

Erich Auerbach feels that a method which disintegrates reality into manifold moments and reflections of consciousness is symptomatic of our contemporary world's sense of helplessness and confusion.[3] That may be true. But it may also be true that so long as there is more than one human nervous system responding to the pandemonium of stimuli which bombard it from birth to death, there will never be a fixed and fast reality. It is precisely because of this that the multiple-point-of-view novel—with its multiplicity of reflection and experience—so eloquently depicts a *Weltansicht* valid for an uncertain world. And because its authors are bid to 'silence', the multiple-point-of-view novel is the product of a literary rhetoric which, in its obscure multiple layers of meaning, stretches language to unprecedented limits of complexity to express the unlimited and the inexpressible.

To develop the ability to read such a novel, then, to be able to handle its many bristly difficulties—some, still unexplored—is to develop a more dynamic perception of the world, to develop a more humane sense of the solemn implications of living, to develop those intuitive powers of judgment which are the very fountainhead of human intercourse. To be able to feel and understand the complex patterns of its intellectual, moral, and emotional evocations is, ultimately, to experience that aesthetic pleasure available to those who have worked to acquire the apprehensive nature of a perfectly cultivated sensibility.

REFERENCE NOTES

CHAPTER ONE

1. *PMLA*, LXX (December, 1955), 1160–84.
2. *Hudson Review* (Spring, 1948), 67–87.
3. *Style in Prose Fiction; English Institute Essays, 1958*, ed. Harold C. Martin (New York, 1959).
4. *Ibid.*, p. 19.
5. *Linguistics and Literary History* (Princeton, 1948), p. 18.
6. *Ibid.*, pp. 135–91.
7. *The Problem of Style* (London, 1922), p. 23.
8. William K. Wimsatt, Jr., *The Prose Style of Samuel Johnson* (New Haven, 1941), p. 63.
9. Thomas A. Sebeok, ed. (Cambridge, Mass., 1960).
10. *New Methods for the Study of Literature* (Chicago, 1927).
11. The dates, here and throughout, correspond to the particular editions listed in the Bibliography; they are not necessarily the original dates of publication.

CHAPTER TWO

1. Fillmore H. Sanford, 'Speech and Personality', *Psychological Bulletin* (December, 1942), p. 840.
2. *Shaw: The Style and the Man* (Middletown, 1962), p. 170.
3. *Style in Language*, ed. Thomas A. Sebeok (Cambridge, Mass., 1960), pp. 283–92.
4. *Ibid.*, p. 289.
5. Sanford, *op. cit.*, p. 816.

CHAPTER THREE

1. Karl Beckson and Arthur Ganz, *A Reader's Guide to Literary Terms* (New York, 1960), p. 162.
2. Translated by Constance Garnett.
3. Translated by Francis Steegmuller.
4. Norman Friedman, 'Point of View in Fiction: The Development of a Critical Concept', *PMLA*, LXX (December, 1955), 1160–84; reprinted in Robert Scholes, ed. *Approaches to the Novel* (San Francisco, 1961), p. 130.
5. Italics are mine.
6. Wayne C. Booth, *The Rhetoric of Fiction* (Chicago, 1961), p. 346.

7. Percy Lubbock, *The Craft of Fiction* (London, 1921), p. 147.

8. *Ibid.*, p. 170.

9. *Messages*; cited in Edwin Muir, *The Structure of the Novel* (London, 1928), pp. 119–20.

10. Booth, *op. cit.*, pp. 323–36; for a detailed account of Joyce's method, see the unpublished dissertation (New York University, 1956) by Erwin R. Steinberg, 'The Stream-of-Consciousness Technique in James Joyce's *Ulysses*'.

11. *Mimesis: The Representation of Reality in Western Literature*, trans. Willard Trask (New York, 1953), p. 474.

12. *Ibid.*, p. 472.

13. *Loc. cit.*

14. See Norman Friedman, *op. cit.*, for a similar 'translation'.

CHAPTER FOUR

1. *Stream of Consciousness in the Modern Novel* (Berkeley and Los Angeles, 1962), p. 29: 'Indirect interior monologue is . . . that type of interior monologue in which the omniscient author presents unspoken material as if it were directly from the consciousness of the character and, with commentary and description, guides the reader through it. It differs from direct interior monologue basically in that the author intervenes between the character's psyche and the reader. The author is an on-the-scene guide for the reader. It retains the fundamental quality of interior monologue in that what it presents of consciousness is direct; that is, it is in the idiom and with the peculiarities of the character's psychic processes.'

2. Page numbers (following each quotation), here and throughout the essay, will refer to the Harbrace Modern Classics edition (New York: Harcourt, Brace and Company, 1927).

3. If (13) and (14) were read aloud to someone not having the text before him, there would be no question in the auditor's mind as to who was speaking. One could tentatively say, then, that the visual effect of punctuation—Joyce and Faulkner, both avid practitioners of punctuationless prose—is intimately connected with creating the sense of immediacy and directness commonly associated with the presentation of inner mental states.

4. *Mimesis: The Representation of Reality in Western Literature*, trans. Willard Trask (New York, 1953), p. 472.

REFERENCE NOTES

CHAPTER FIVE

1. Virginia Woolf, 'Modern Fiction', *Modern British Fiction: Essays in Criticism*, ed. Mark Schorer (New York, 1961), p. 9.
2. *Ibid.*, pp. 5–6.
3. *Ibid.*, p. 7.
4. 'Virginia Woolf: The Poetic Method', *The Symposium*, III (1932), 56.
5. *Virginia Woolf* (Norfolk, Connecticut, 1942), p. 84.
6. Italics are mine.
7. The Omniscient Narrator was discussed in an earlier chapter; Mrs McNab's role is self-evident as a *persona*; and Cam, though her lines amount to the same as James', is subordinate to him as a character and was, therefore, not considered significant enough a narrator to analyse critically. Her most important role in the novel becomes apparent only in its third section. Here, the love Cam expresses for her father not only works to point up James' persistent antagonism towards him, but also functions to make James' final relationship to his new-found father all the more dramatic and poignant.
8. Elizabeth Drew, *The Novel: A Modern Guide to Fifteen English Masterpieces* (New York, 1963), p. 269.
9. *Ibid.*, p. 277.
10. *Virginia Woolf: A Commentary* (London, 1949), p. 104.
11. *Ibid.*, p. 102.
12. *Ibid.*, p. 110; italics are mine.
13. *Ibid.*, p. 123.
14. *Ibid.*, p. 113.
15. Berkeley and Los Angeles, 1954.
16. Hafley, *op. cit.*, p. 80.
17. Cambridge, 1964, second edition, pp. 80–1.
18. Bennett, *op. cit.*, p. 81.
19. *Aspects of the Novel* (New York, 1927), p. 27.
20. Drew, *op. cit.*, pp. 278–9.
21. 'Spatial Form in Modern Literature', reprinted from *Sewanee Review* in *Criticism: The Foundations of Modern Literary Judgment*, ed. Schorer, Miles, McKenzie (New York, 1958), revised edition, p. 384.
22. 'The Waters of Annihilation: Double Vision in *To the Lighthouse*', *Journal of English Literary History*, XXII, No. 2 (1955), 61–79.
23. *The Common Reader: First and Second Series* (New York, 1948), pp. 88–9.
24. For a similar, though less detailed and differently

oriented, discussion, see Glenn Pederson, 'Vision in *To the Lighthouse*', *PMLA*, LXXIII, No. 5 (1958), 585–600.

25. Not all nineteen references are discussed here. Anyone wishing to develop further this line of analysis will find the hedge mentioned on pp. 32, 33, 41, 52, 56, 66, 67, 68, 82, 84, 98, 99, 221, 223, 234, 269, 287, and 294.

26. See p. 234: the greens and blues become the hedge's equivalent.

27. Susanne K. Langer, *Philosophy in a New Key: A Study in the Symbolism of Reason, Rite, and Art* (Cambridge, Mass., 1957), p. 75.

CHAPTER SIX

1. Although more recent definitions of the sentence have tended to replace this traditional one, I have used it because it allows for the greatest consistency among all the samples.

2. It might be noted parenthetically, that over extended passages (and even to a lesser extent in these 840-word samples) the thoughts and utterances of Mr Ramsay, the Omniscient Narrator, and Lily Briscoe emerge as the most aesthetically satisfying, lyrical prose when compared with that of the other narrators.

3. 'Generative Grammars and the Concept of Literary Style', *Word* (December, 1964), 436–7.

4. The terms 'Content' and 'Structural' come from Edith Rickert, *New Methods for the Study of Literature* (Chicago, 1927), p. 74. Content words, according to Rickert, refer to nouns, verbs (except copulative and auxiliary), descriptive adjectives, and descriptive adverbs. Structural words refer to pronouns, copulative and auxiliary verbs, limiting adjectives (relative, demonstrative, interrogative, and some indefinite adjectives), articles, limiting and conjunctive adverbs (adverbs of degree, of indefinite time and place, relative and conjunctive adverbs), prepositions, conjunctions, and interjections. Content words convey ideas, and structural words show relationships. In more recent terminology (see W. Nelson Francis, *The Structure of American English*, New York, 1958), structural words are roughly equivalent to *function words*, and content words to *lexical words*. The content and structural words for all of the samples have been isolated and treated statistically in Appendix B.

5. In cases of doubt whether a participle should be considered a verbal or an adjectival, the rule of thumb suggested by James Sledd (*A Short Introduction to English Grammar*, Chicago, 1959, p. 91) was used: 'Substitute other forms in the doubtful

position to see whether it can be regularly filled by both adjectives and participles or by participles only. If both adjectives and participles can regularly be substituted, then the doubtful participle is an adjectival; otherwise it is a verbal.'

6. *Style in Language,* ed. Thomas A. Sebeok (Cambridge, Mass., 1960), pp. 283–92. In this study, 150 passages from various sources of nineteenth- and twentieth-century English prose were analysed. Carroll's objective scale was developed from the initial factor analysis performed by means of Thurstone's centroid method; and its validity was demonstrated in his 'Biquartimin Criterion for Rotation to Oblique Simple Structure in Factor Analysis', *Science* 126. 1114–15 (1957).

7. Sebeok, p. 290.

8. *Shakespeare's Imagery and What it Tells Us* (Cambridge, 1935), Appendix VII.

9. *Principles of Literary Criticism* (London, 1930), p. 119.

10. Rosemond Tuve, 'The Criterion of Rhetorical Efficacy', *Elizabethan and Metaphysical Imagery* (Chicago, 1947), pp. 180–191.

11. Italics are mine.

CHAPTER SEVEN

1. See Louise M. Rosenblatt, *Literature as Exploration* (New York, 1968), revised edition, pp. 25–53.

2. Martin Steinmann, Jr., 'The Old Novel and the New', *From Jane Austen to Joseph Conrad,* ed. Robert C. Rathburn and Martin Steinmann, Jr. (Minneapolis, 1958), pp. 286–306.

3. *Mimesis: The Representation of Reality in Western Literature,* trans. Willard Trask (New York, 1953), p. 487.

APPENDIX A

In the samples which follow, the sentences are broken down into their clausal components by means of brackets. In the notation following each opening bracket (in parentheses), the letter(s) classifies the clause type; and the Arabic numeral which follows indicates the level at which the clause is embedded.

KEY TO CLAUSE TYPES

Main:	M
Adjective:	A
Adverb:	Av
Parenthetical:	P
Noun:	N

Words which have been lined out are those which belong to a narrator other than the one whose name heads the sample.

Mrs Ramsay
(pp. 88–92)

1 . . . [(M) a woman had once accused her of 'robbing her of her daughter's affections';] [(M) something [A-1) Mrs Doyle had said] made her remember that charge again.]

2 [(M) Wishing to dominate, wishing to interfere, making people do [(N-1) what she wished]—that was the charge against her,] and [(M) she thought it most unjust.]

3 [(M) How could she help being 'like that' to look at?]

4 [(M) No one could accuse her of taking pains to impress.]

5 [(M) She was often ashamed of her own shabbiness.]

6 [(M) Nor was she domineering,] [(M) nor was she tyrannical.]

7 [(M) It was more true about hospitals and drains and the dairy.]

8 [(M) About things like that she did feel passionately, and would [(Av-1) if she had had the chance,] have liked to take people by the scruff of their necks and make them see.]

9 No hospital on the whole island.

10 [(M) It was a disgrace.]

11 Milk delivered at your door in London positively brown with dirt.

12 [(M) It should be made illegal.]

13 [(M) A model dairy and a hospital up here—those two things she would have liked to do, herself.]

14 But how?

15 With all these children?

16 [(M) [(Av-1) When they were older,] then perhaps she would have time; [(Av-1) when they were all at school.]]

17 [(M) Oh, but she never wanted James to grow a day older! or Cam either.]

18 [(M) These two she would have liked to keep for ever [(Av-1) just as they were, demons of wickedness, angels of delight,] never to see them grow up into long-legged monsters.]

19 [(M) Nothing made up for the loss.]

20 [(M) [(Av-1) When she read just now to James, 'and there were numbers of soldiers with kettledrums and trumpets,' and his eyes darkened,] she thought, [(N-1) why should they grow up, and lose all that?]]

21 [(M) He was the most gifted, the most sensitive of her children.]

22 [(M) [(N-1) But all, she thought, were full of promise.]]

23 [(M) Prue, a perfect angel with the others, and sometimes now, at night especially, she took one's breath away with her beauty.]

24 [(M) Andrew—even her husband admitted [(N-1) that his gift for mathematics was extraordinary.]]

25 [(M) And Nancy and Roger, they were both wild creatures now, scampering about over the country all day long.]

26 [(M) As for Rose, her mouth was too big,] but [(M) she had a wonderful gift with her hands.]

27 [(M) [(Av-1) If they had charades,] Rose made the dresses; made everything; liked best arranging tables, flowers, anything.]

28 [(M) She did not like it [(A-1) that Jasper should shoot birds;]] [(M) but it was only a stage;] [(M) they all went through stages.]

29 [(M) [(N-1) Why, she asked, ~~pressing her chin on James's head~~, should they grow up so fast?]]

30 [(M) Why should they go to school?]

31 [(M) She would have liked always to have a baby.]

32 [(M) She was happiest carrying one in her arms.]

33 [(M) Then people might say [(N-1) she was tyrannical, domineering, masterful,] [(Av-1) if they chose;]] [(M) she did not mind.]

34 [(M) And, ~~touching his hair with her lips~~, she thought, [(N-1) he will never be so happy again,] but stopped herself, remembering [(N-1) how it angered her husband [(N-2) that she should say that.]]]

35 [(M) Still, it was true.]

36 [(M) They were happier now [(Av-1) than they would ever be again.]]

37 [(M) A tenpenny tea set made Cam happy for days.]

38 [(M) She heard them stamping and crowing on the floor above her head the moment [(A-1) they woke.]]

39 [(M) They came bustling along the passage.]

40 [(M) Then the door sprang open] and [(M) in they came, fresh as roses, staring, wide awake, [(Av-1) as if this coming into the dining-room after breakfast, [A-2) which they did every day of their lives,] was a positive event to them,] and so on, with one thing after another, all day long, [(Av-1) until she went up

to say good-night to them, and found them netted in
their cots like birds among cherries and raspberries,
still making up stories about some little bit of rubbish—something [(A-2) they had heard,] something
[(A-2) they had picked up in the garden.]]]

41 [(M) They had all their little treasures. . . .]

42 [(M) And so she went down and said to her husband,
[(N-1) Why must they grow up and lose it all?]]

43 [(M) Never will they be so happy again.]

44 [(M) And he was angry.]

45 [(M) [(N-1) Why take such a gloomy view of life?]
he said.]

46 [(M) It is not sensible.]

47 [(M) For it was odd;] [(M) and she believed it to be
true; [(N-1) that with all his gloom and desperation
he was happier, more hopeful on the whole, [(Av-2)
than she was.]]]

48 [(M) Less exposed to human worries—perhaps that
was it.]

49 [(M) He had always his work to fall back on.]

50 [(M) Not that she herself was 'pessimistic', [(Av-1) as
he accused her of being.]]

51 [(M) Only she thought life]—and [(M) a little strip
of time presented itself to her eyes—her fifty years.]

52 [(M) There it was before her—life.]

53 [(M) . . . [(N-1) there were, she remembered, great
reconciliation scenes;]] [(M) but for the most part,
oddly enough, she must admit [(N-1) that she felt
this thing [(A-2) that she called life] terrible, hostile,
and quick to pounce on you [(Av-2) if you gave it a
chance.]]]

54 [(M) There were the eternal problems; suffering;
death; the poor.]

55 [(M) There was always a woman dying of cancer even
here.]

56 [(M) And yet she had said to all these children,
[(N-1) You shall go through it all.]]

57 [(M) To eight people she had said relentlessly that

[(P-1) (and the bill for the greenhouse would be fifty pounds).]]

58 [(M) For that reason, knowing [(N-1) what was before them—love and ambition and being wretched alone in dreary places—] she had often the feeling, [(N-1) Why must* they grow up and lose it all?]]

* 840 words.

Mr Ramsay
(pp. 54–7)

1 [(M) The geranium in the urn became startlingly visible] and, [(M) displayed among its leaves, he could see, without wishing it, that old, that obvious distinction between the two classes of men; on the one hand the steady goers of superhuman strength [(A-1) who, plodding and persevering, repeat the whole alphabet in order, twenty-six letters in all, from start to finish;] on the other the gifted, the inspired [(A-1) who, miraculously, lump all the letters together in one flash—the way of genius.]]

2 [(M) He had not genius;] [(M) he laid no claim to that;] [(M) but he had, or might have had, the power to repeat every letter of the alphabet from A to Z accurately in order.]

3 [(M) Meanwhile, he stuck at Q.]

4 On, then, on to R.

5 [(M) Feelings [(A-1) that would not have disgraced a leader [(A-2) who, [(Av-3) now that the snow has begun to fall and the mountain top is covered in mist,] knows [(N-3) that he must lay himself down and die [(A-4) before morning comes,]]]]] stole over upon him,] ~~paling the colour of his eyes, giving him, even in the two minutes of his turn on the terrace, the bleached look of withered old age.~~

6 [(M) Yet he would not die lying down;] [(M) he

would find some crag of rock,] and [(M) there, his eyes fixed on the storm, trying to the end to pierce the darkness, he would die standing.]

7 [(M) He would never reach R.]

8 [(M) He 'stood stock-still, by the urn, with the geranium flowing over it.]

9 [(M) [(N-1) How many men in a thousand million, he asked himself, reach Z after all?]]

10 [(M) Surely the leader of a forlorn hope may ask himself that and answer, without treachery to the expedition behind him, 'One perhaps'.]

11 One in a generation.

12 [(M) Is he to be blamed then [(Av-1) if he is not that one?] [(Av-1) provided he has toiled honestly, given to the best of his power, and till he has no more left to give?]]

13 [(M) And his fame lasts how long?]

14 [(M) It is permissible even for a dying hero to think [(Av-1) before he dies] [(N-1) how men will speak of him hereafter.]]

15 [(M) His fame lasts perhaps two thousand years.]

16 [(M) And what arc two thousand years?] (~~asked Mr Ramsay ironically, staring at the hedge~~).

17 What, indeed, [(Av-1) if you look from a mountain top down the long wastes of the ages?]

18 [(M) The very stone [(A-1) one kicks with one's boot] will outlast Shakespeare.]

19 [(M) His own little light would shine, not very brightly, for a year or two, and would then be merged in some bigger light, and that in a bigger still.] (~~He looked into the hedge, into the intricacy of the twigs.~~)

20 [(M) Who then could blame the leader of that forlorn party [(A-1) which after all has climbed high enough to see the waste of the years and the perishing of stars,] [(Av-1) if [(Av-2) before death stiffens his limbs beyond the power of movement] he does a little consciously raise his numbed fingers to his brow, and

square his shoulders, [(Av-2) so that [(Av-3) when the search party comes] they will find him dead at his post, the fine figure of a soldier?]]] M̶r̶ R̶a̶m̶s̶a̶y̶ s̶q̶u̶a̶r̶e̶d̶ h̶i̶s̶ s̶h̶o̶u̶l̶d̶e̶r̶s̶ a̶n̶d̶ s̶t̶o̶o̶d̶ v̶e̶r̶y̶ u̶p̶r̶i̶g̶h̶t̶ b̶y̶ t̶h̶e̶ u̶r̶n̶.

21 [(M) Who shall blame him, [(Av-1) if, so standing for a moment, he dwells upon fame, upon search parties, upon cairns raised by grateful followers over his bones?]]

22 [(M) Finally, who shall blame the leader of the doomed expedition, [(Av-1) if, having adventured to the uttermost, and used his strength wholly to the last ounce and fallen asleep not much caring [(N-2) if he wakes or not,] he now perceives by some pricking in his toes [(N-2) that he lives,] and does not on the whole object to live, but requires sympathy, and whisky, and some one to tell the story of his suffering to at once?]]

23 [(M) Who shall blame him?]

24 [(M) Who will not secretly rejoice [(Av-1) when the hero puts his armour off, and halts by the window and gazes at his wife and son, [(A-2) who, very distant at first, gradually come closer and closer, [(Av-3) till lips and book and head are clearly before him,] though still lovely and. unfamiliar from the intensity of his isolation and the waste of ages and the perishing of the stars,]]] and [(M) finally p̶u̶t̶t̶i̶n̶g̶ h̶i̶s̶ p̶i̶p̶e̶ i̶n̶ h̶i̶s̶ p̶o̶c̶k̶e̶t̶ a̶n̶d̶ b̶e̶n̶d̶i̶n̶g̶ h̶i̶s̶ m̶a̶g̶n̶i̶f̶i̶c̶e̶n̶t̶ h̶e̶a̶d̶ b̶e̶f̶o̶r̶e̶ h̶e̶r̶—who will blame him [(Av-1) if he does homage to the beauty of the world?]]

(pp. 69-70)

25 [(M) 'But the father of eight children has no choice.'] M̶u̶t̶t̶e̶r̶i̶n̶g̶ h̶a̶l̶f̶ a̶l̶o̶u̶d̶, s̶o̶ h̶e̶ b̶r̶o̶k̶e̶ o̶f̶f̶, t̶u̶r̶n̶e̶d̶, s̶i̶g̶h̶e̶d̶, r̶a̶i̶s̶e̶d̶ h̶i̶s̶ e̶y̶e̶s̶, s̶o̶u̶g̶h̶t̶ t̶h̶e̶ f̶i̶g̶u̶r̶e̶ o̶f̶ h̶i̶s̶ w̶i̶f̶e̶ r̶e̶a̶d̶i̶n̶g̶ s̶t̶o̶r̶i̶e̶s̶ t̶o̶ h̶i̶s̶ l̶i̶t̶t̶l̶e̶ b̶o̶y̶, f̶i̶l̶l̶e̶d̶ h̶i̶s̶ p̶i̶p̶e̶.

26 [(M) He turned from the sight of human ignorance and human fate and the sea eating the ground [(A-1)

we stand on,] [(A-1) which, [(Av-2) had he been able to contemplate it fixedly] might have led to something;]] ~~and found consolation in trifles so slight compared with the august theme just now before him that he was disposed to slur that comfort over, to deprecate it, as if to be caught happy in a world of misery was for an honest man the most despicable of crimes.~~

27 [(M) It was true;] [(M) he was for the most part happy;] [(M) he had his wife;] [(M) he had his children;] [(M) he had promised in six weeks' time to talk 'some nonsense' to the young men of Cardiff about Locke, Hume, Berkeley, and the causes of the French Revolution.]

28 But this and his pleasure in it, his glory in the phrases [(A-1) he made,] in the ardour of youth, in his wife's beauty, in the tributes [(A-1) that reached him from Swansea, Cardiff, Exeter, Southampton, Kidderminster, Oxford, Cambridge—]

(pp. 98–9)

29 . . . [(M) he could not help noting, ~~as he passed,~~ the sternness at the heart of her beauty.]

30 [(M) It saddened him,] and [(M) her remoteness pained him,] and [(M) he felt, ~~as he passed,~~ [(N-1) that he could not protect her,]] and, [(M) [(Av-1) when he reached the hedge,] he was sad.]

31 [(M) He could do nothing to help her.]

32 [(M) He must stand by and watch her.]

33 [(N-1) Indeed, [(M) the infernal truth was,] he made things worse for her.]

34 [(M) He was irritable—] [(M) he was touchy.]

35 [(M) He had lost his temper over the Lighthouse.] . . .

(p. 100)

36 [(M) . . . [(N-1) Ah! She was lovely, lovelier* now than ever,] he thought.]

* 840 words.

James Ramsay
(pp. 273-8)

1 [(M) And James felt [(N-1) that each page was turned
with a peculiar gesture aimed at him: now assertively,
now commandingly; now with the intention of making
people pity him;]] [(M) and all the time, [(Av-1) as
his father read and turned one after another of those
little pages,] James kept dreading the moment [(A-1)
when he would look up and speak sharply to him
about something or other.]]

2 [(M) [(N-1) Why were they lagging about here?] he
would demand, or something quite unreasonable like
that.]

3 [(M) [(Av-1) And [(Av-2) if he does,] James thought,
then I shall take a knife and strike him to the
heart.]] . . .

4 [(M) Only now, ~~as he grew older, and sat staring at
his father in an impotent rage,~~ it was not him, that
old man reading, [(A-1) whom he wanted to kill,]]
but [(M) it was the thing [(A-1) that descended on
him]—~~without his knowing it perhaps~~: that fierce
sudden black-winged harpy, with its talons and its
beak all cold and hard, [(A-1) that struck and struck
at you [(P-2) (he could feel the beak on his bare legs,
[(A-3) where it had struck [(Av-4) when he was a
child)]]] and then made off,]] and [(M) there he was
again, an old man, very sad, reading his book.]

5 [(M) That he would kill,] [(M) that he would strike
to the heart.]

6 [(M) [(Av-1) Whatever he did]—[(P-1) (and [(N-2)
he might do anything,] he felt,] ~~looking at the Lighthouse and the distant shore~~) [(Av-1)) whether he
was in a business, in a bank, a barrister, a man at the
head of some enterprise,] that he would fight,] [(M)
that he would track down and stamp out]—[(M)
tyranny, despotism, he called it—making people do

[(N-1) what they did not want to do,] cutting off their right to speak.]

7 [(M) How could any of them say, [(N-1) But I won't,] [(Av-1) when he said, [(N-2) Come to the Lighthouse.]]]

8 [(M) Do this.]

9 [(M) Fetch me that.]

10 [(M) The black wings spread,] and [(M) the hard beak tore.]

11 [(M) And the next moment, there he sat reading his book;] and [(M) he might look up—[(P-1) one never knew]—quite reasonably.]

12 [(M) He might talk to the Macalisters.]

13 [(M) [(N-1) He might be pressing a sovereign into some frozen old woman's hand in the street,] James thought, and [(N-1) he might be shouting out at some fisherman's sports;] [(N-1) he might be waving his arms in the air with excitement.]]

14 [(M) Or he might sit at the head of the table dead silent from one end of dinner to the other.]

15 [(M) Yes, thought James, ~~while the boat slapped and dawdled there in the hot sun~~; [(N-1) there was a waste of snow and rock very lonely and austere;]] and [(M) there he had come to feel, quite often lately, [(Av-1) when his father said something or did something [(A-2) which surprised the others,]] [(N-1) there were two pairs of footprints only; his own and his father's.]]

16 [(M) They alone knew each other.]

17 [(M) What then was this terror, this hatred?] . . .

18 [(M) Suppose then [(N-1) that as a child sitting helpless in a perambulator, or on someone's knee, he had seen a waggon crush ignorantly and innocently, some one's foot?]]

19 [(M) Suppose [(N-1) he had seen the foot first, in the grass, smooth, and whole; then the wheel; and the same foot, purple, crushed.]]

20 [(M) But the wheel was innocent.]

21 [(M) So now, [(Av-1) when his father came striding down the passage knocking them up early in the morning to go to the Lighthouse] down it came over his foot, over Cam's foot, over anybody's foot.]

22 [(M) One sat and watched it.]

23 [(M) But whose foot was he thinking of,] and [(M) in what garden did all this happen?]

24 [(M) For one had settings for these scenes; trees [(A-1) that grew there;] flowers; a certain light; a few figures.]

25 [(M) Everything tended to set itself in a garden [(A-1) where there was none of this gloom.]]

26 None of this throwing of hands about; [(M) people spoke in an ordinary tone of voice.]

27 [(M) They went in and out all day long.]

28 [(M) There was an old woman gossiping in the kitchen;] [(M) and the blinds were sucked in and out by the breeze;] [(M) all was blowing,] [(M) all was growing;] [(M) and over all those plates and bowls and tall brandishing red and yellow flowers a very thin yellow veil would be drawn, like a vine leaf, at night.]

29 [(M) Things became stiller and darker at night.]

30 [(M) But the leaf-like veil was so fine, [(Av-1) that lights lifted it,] [(Av-1) voices crinkled it;]] [(M) he could see through it a figure stooping, hear, coming close, going away, some dress rustling, some chain tinkling.]

31 [(M) It was in this world [(A-1) that the wheel went over the person's foot.]]

32 [(M) [(N-1) Something, he remembered, stayed and darkened over him; would not move;] [(N-1) something flourished up in the air,] [(N-1) something arid and sharp descended even there, like a blade, a scimitar, smiting through the leaves and flowers even of that happy world and making it shrivel and fall.]]

33 'It will rain,' [(M) he remembered his father saying.] 'You won't be able to go to the Lighthouse.'

34 [(M) The Lighthouse was then a silvery, misty-looking tower with a yellow eye, [(A-1) that opened suddenly, and softly in the evening.]]

35 Now—~~James looked at the Lighthouse.~~

36 [(M) He could see the white-washed rocks; the tower, stark and straight;] [(M) he could see [(N-1) that it was barred with black and white;]] [(M) he could see windows in it;] [(M) he could even see washing spread on the rocks to dry.]

37 [(M) So that was the Lighthouse, [(P-1) was it?]]

38 [(M) No, the other was also the Lighthouse.]

39 [(M) For nothing was simply one thing.]

40 [(M) The other Lighthouse was true too.]

Cam Ramsay

(pp. 280–4)

1 [(M) [(N-1) It was like that then, the island,] thought Cam,] ~~once more drawing her fingers through the waves. She had never seen it from out at sea before.~~

2 [(M) It lay like that on the sea, [(P-1) did it,] with a dent in the middle and two sharp crags,] and [(M) the sea swept in there, and spread away for miles on either side of the island.]

3 [(M) It was very small; shaped something like a leaf stood on end.]

4 [(M) [(N-1) So we took a little boat,] she thought, beginning to tell herself a story of adventure about escaping from a sinking ship.]

5 ~~But with the sea streaming through her fingers, a spray of seaweed vanishing behind them, she did not want to tell herself seriously a story; it was the sense of adventure and escape that she wanted, for~~ [(M) she was thinking, ~~as the boat sailed on,~~ [(N-1) how her father's anger about the points of the compass, James' obstinacy about the compact, and her own anguish, all had slipped,] [(N-1) all had passed,] [(N-1) all had streamed away.]]

6 [(M) What then came next?]

7 [(M) Where were they going?] . . .

8 [(M) [(N-1) Small [(Av-2) as it was,] and shaped something like a leaf stood on its end with the gold-sprinkled waters flowing in and about it, it had, she supposed, a place in the universe—even that little island?]]

9 [(M) [(N-1) The old gentleman in the study she thought could have told her.]]

10 [(M) Sometimes she strayed in from the garden purposely to catch them at it.]

11 [(M) There they were [(P-1) (it might be Mr Carmichael or Mr Bankes [(A-2) who was sitting with her father)]] sitting opposite each other in their low arm-chairs.]

12 [(M) They were crackling in front of them the pages of *The Times*, [(Av-1) when she came in from the garden, all in a muddle, about something [(A-2) some one had said about Christ,] or hearing [(N-2) that a mammoth had been dug up in a London street,] or wondering [(N-2) what Napoleon was like.]]]

13 [(M) Then they took all this with their clean hands [(P-1) (they wore grey-coloured clothes;] [(P-1) they smelt of heather)]] and [(M) they brushed the scraps together, turning the paper, crossing their knees, and said something now and then very brief.]

14 [(M) Just to please herself she would take a book from the shelf and stand there, watching her father write so equally, so neatly from one side of the page to another, with a little cough now and then, or something said briefly to the other old gentleman opposite.]

15 [(M) And she thought, ~~standing there with her book open~~, [(N-1) one could let [(N-2) whatever one thought] expand here like a leaf in water;]] [(M) and [(Av-1) if it did well here, among the old gentlemen smoking and *The Times* crackling] then it was right.]

16 ~~And watching her father as he wrote in his study,~~

[(M) she thought (~~now sitting in the boat~~) [(N-1) he was not vain, nor a tyrant and did not wish to make you pity him.]]

17 [(M) Indeed, [(Av-1) if he saw [(N-2) she was there, reading a book,]] he would ask her, [(Av-1) as gently as any one could,] [(N-1) Was there nothing [(A-2) he could give her?]]]

18 [(M) [(Av-1) Lest this should be wrong,] she looked at him reading the little book with the shiny cover mottled like a plover's egg.]

19 No; [(M) it was right.]

20 [(M) [(N-1) Look at him now,] she wanted to say aloud to James.] (~~But James had his eye on the sail.~~)

21 [(M) [(N-1) He is a sarcastic brute,] James would say.]

22 [(M) [(N-1) He brings the talk round to himself and his books,] James would say.]

23 [(M) He is intolerably egotistical.]

24 [(M) Worst of all, he is a tyrant.]

25 [(M) [(N-1) But look!] she said,] ~~looking at him.~~

26 [(M) Look at him now.]

27 [(M) She looked at him reading the little book with his legs curled; the little book [(A-1) whose yellowish pages she knew, without knowing [(N-2) what was written on them.]]]

28 [(M) It was small;] [(M) it was closely printed;] [(M) on the fly-leaf, she knew, [(N-1) he had written [(N-2) that he had spent fifteen francs on dinner;] [(N-2) the wine had been so much;] [(N-2) he had given so much to the waiter;]]] [(M) all was added up neatly at the bottom of the page.]

29 [(M) But [(N-1) what might be written in the book [(A-2) which had rounded its edges off in his pocket,]] she did not know.] . . .

30 [(M) [(N-1) He read, she thought, [(Av-2) as if he were guiding something, or wheedling a large flock of sheep, or pushing his way up and up a single narrow path;]] [(N-1) and sometimes he went fast and

straight, and broke his way through the bramble,]
and [(N-1) sometimes it seemed [(N-2) a branch
struck at him, a bramble blinded him, but he was not
going to let himself be beaten by that;]]] [(M) on he
went, tossing over page after page.]

31 [(M) And she went on telling herself a story about
escaping from a sinking ship, [(Av-1) for she was
safe, [(Av-2) while he sat there;] safe, [(Av-2) as she
felt herself [(Av-3) when she crept in from the garden,
and took a book down, and the old gentlemen,
lowering the paper suddenly, said something very
brief over the top of it about the character of
Napoleon.]]]]

32 [(M) She gazed back over the sea, at the island.]

33 [(M) But the leaf was losing its sharpness.]

34 [(M) It was very small;] [(M) it was very distant.]

35 [(M) The sea was more important now than the
shore.] . . .

36 [(M) About here, she thought, ~~dabbling her fingers in
the water~~, [(N-1) a ship had sunk,]] and [(M) she
murmured, ~~dreamily half asleep~~, [(N-1) how we
perished, each alone.]]

(pp. 302–3)

37 [(M) [(N-1) It was thus [(A-2) that he escaped,]] she
thought.]

38 [(M) Yes, with his great forehead and his great nose,
holding his little mottled book firmly in front of him,
he escaped.]

39 [(M) You might try to lay hands on him,] but [(M)
then like a bird, he spread his wings,] [(M) he floated
off to settle out of your reach somewhere far away on
some desolate stump.] . . .

40 [(M) The island had* grown so small [(Av-1) that it
scarcely looked like a leaf any longer.]]

* 840 words.

APPENDIX A

Omniscient Narrator

(pp. 189–93)

1 [(M) So with the lamps all put out, the moon sunk,
and the thin rain drumming on the roof, a downpouring of immense darkness began.]

2 [(M) Nothing, [(P-1) it seemed,] could survive the
flood, the profusion of darkness [(A-1) which, creeping in at keyholes and crevices, stole round window
blinds, came into bedrooms, swallowed up here a jug
and basin, there a bowl of red and yellow dahlias,
there the sharp edges and firm bulk of a chest of
drawers.]]

3 [(M) Not only was furniture confounded;] [(M) there
was scarcely anything left of body or mind [(A-1)
by which one could say, [(N-2) 'This is he'] or
[(N-2) 'This is she.']]]

4 [(M) Sometimes a hand was raised as if to clutch
something or ward off something,] or [(M) somebody groaned,] or [(M) somebody laughed aloud as
if sharing a joke with nothingness.]

5 [(M) Nothing stirred in the drawing-room or in the
dining-room or on the staircase.]

6 [(M) Only through the rusty hinges and swollen sea-
moistened woodwork certain airs, detached from the
body of the wind [(P-1) (the house was ramshackle
after all)] crept round corners and ventured indoors.]

7 [(M) Almost one might imagine them, [(Av-1) as they
entered the drawing-room questioning and wondering, toying with the flap of hanging wall-paper, asking, [(N-2) would it hang much longer,] [(N-2) when
would it fall?]]]

8 [(M) Then smoothly brushing the walls, they passed
on musingly as if asking the red and yellow roses on
the wall-paper [(N-1) whether they would fade,] and
questioning (gently, [(P-1) for there was time at their
disposal]) the torn letters in the waste-paper basket,

185

the flowers, the books, all of [(N-1) which were now
open to them] and asking, [(N-1) Were they allies?]
[(N-1) Were they enemies?] [(N-1) How long would
they endure?]]

9 [(M) So some random light directing them with its
pale footfall upon stair and mat, from some uncovered
star, or wandering ship, or the Lighthouse even, the
little airs mounted the staircase and nosed round bedroom doors.]

10 [(M) But here surely, they must cease.]

11 [(M) [(Av-1) Whatever else may perish and disappear,] [(N-1) what lies here] is steadfast.]

12 [(M) Here one might say to those sliding lights, those
fumbling airs [(A-1) that breathe and bend over the
bed itself,] [(N-1) here you can neither touch nor
destroy.]]

13 [(M) Upon which, wearily, ghostlily, [(Av-1) as if
they had feather-light fingers and the light persistency of feathers,] they would look, once, on the
shut eyes, and the loosely clasping fingers, and fold
their garments wearily and disappear.]

14 [(M) And so, nosing, rubbing, they went to the window on the staircase, to the servants' bedrooms, to the
boxes in the attics; descending, blanched the apples
on the dining-room table, fumbled the petals of roses,
tried the picture on the easel, brushed the mat and
blew a little sand along the floor.]

15 [(M) At length, desisting, all ceased together, gathered
together,] [(M) all sighed together;] [(M) all together gave off an aimless gust of lamentation [(Av-1)
to which some door in the kitchen replied; swung
wide; admitted nothing; and slammed to.]]

16 [[(M) Here Mr Carmichael, [(A-1) who was reading
Virgil,] blew out his candle.]

17 [(M) It was midnight.]]

18 [(M) But what after all is one night?]

19 A short space, especially [(Av-1) when the darkness
dims so soon, and so soon a bird sings, a cock crows,

or a faint green quickens, like a turning leaf, in the hollow of the wave.]

20 [(M) Night, however, succeeds to night.]

21 [(M) The winter holds a pack of them in store and deals them equally, evenly, with indefatigable fingers.]

22 [(M) They lengthen;] [(M) they darken.]

23 [(M) Some of them hold aloft clear planets, plates of brightness.]

24 [(M) The autumn trees, ravaged [(Av-1) as they are] take on the flash of tattered flags kindling in the gloom of cool cathedral caves [(A-1) where gold letters on marble pages describe death in battle and [(N-2) how bones bleach and burn far away in Indian sands.]]]

25 [(M) The autumn trees gleam in the yellow moonlight, in the light of harvest moons, the light [(A-1) which mellows the energy of labour, and smooths the stubble, and brings the wave lapping blue to the shore.]]

26 [(M) It seemed now [(N-1) as if, touched by human penitence and all its toil, divine goodness had parted the curtain and displayed behind it, single, distinct, the hare erect; the wave falling; the boat rocking, [(A-2) which, [(Av-3) did we deserve them,] should be ours always.]]]

27 [(M) But alas, divine goodness, twitching the cord, draws the curtain;] [(M) it does not please him;] [(M) he covers his treasures in a drench of hail, and so breaks them, so confuses them [(Av-1) that it seems impossible [(N-2) that their calm should ever return] or [(N-2) that we should ever compose from their fragments a perfect whole or read in the littered pieces the clear words of truth.]]]

28 [(M) For our penitence deserves a glimpse only; our toil respite only.]

29 [(M) The nights are now full of wind and destruction;] [(M) the trees plunge and bend] and [(M) their

leaves fly helter skelter [(Av-1) until the lawn is plastered with them and they lie packed in gutters and choke rain pipes and scatter damp paths.]]

30 [(M) Also the sea tosses itself and breaks itself,] and [(M) [(Av-1) should any sleeper fancying [(N-1) that he might find on the beach an answer to his doubts, a sharer of his solitude,] throw off* his bedclothes and go down by himself to walk on the sand,] no image with semblance of serving and divine promptitude comes readily to hand bringing the night to order and making the world reflect the compass of the soul.]

   * 840 words.

William Bankes

(p. 31)

1 [(M) [(N-1) Her shoes were excellent,] he observed.]
2 [(M) They allowed the toes their natural expansion.]
3 [(M) Lodging in the same house with her, he had noticed too, [(N-1) how orderly she was, up before breakfast and off to paint, [(P-2) he believed,] alone: poor, presumably, and without the complexion or the allurement of Miss Doyle certainly, but with a good sense [(A-2) which made her in his eyes superior to that young lady.]]]
4 [(M) [(N-1) Now, for instance, [(Av-2) when Ramsay bore down on them, shouting, gesticulating,] Miss Briscoe, he felt certain, understood.]]

(pp. 34–6)

5 [(M) William Bankes thought of Ramsay: thought of a road in Westmoreland, thought of Ramsay striding along a road by himself hung round with that solitude [(A-1) which seemed to be his natural air.]]
6 [(M) [(N-1) But this was suddenly interrupted, William Bankes remembered (and this must refer to some actual incident), by a hen, straddling her wings

out in protection of a covey of little chicks, [(Av-2)
upon which, Ramsay, stopping, pointed his stick and
said 'Pretty—pretty,' an odd illumination in to his
heart, [(P-3) Bankes had thought it,] [(A-3) which
showed his simplicity, his sympathy with humble
things;]]]] [(M) but it seemed to him [(N-1) as if
their friendship had ceased, there, on that stretch of
road.]]

7 [(M) After that, Ramsay had married.]

8 [(M) After that, what with one thing and another, the
pulp had gone out of their friendship.]

9 [(M) [(N-1) Whose fault it was] he could not say,]
[(M)only, after a time, repetition had taken the place
of newness.]

10 [(M) It was to repeat [(N-1) that they met.]]

11 But in this dumb colloquy with the sand dunes [(M)
he maintained [(N-1) that his affection for Ramsay
had in no way diminished;]] but [(M) there, like
the body of a young man laid up in peat for a century, with the red fresh on his lips, was his friendship,
in its acuteness and reality, laid up across the bay
among the sandhills.]

12 [(M) He was anxious for the sake of this friendship and .
perhaps too in order to clear himself in his own mind
from the imputation of having dried and shrunk]
—for Ramsay lived in a welter of children, whereas
Bankes was childless and a widower—[(M) he was
anxious [(N-1) that Lily Briscoe should not disparage Ramsay (a great man in his own way) yet
should understand [(N-2) how things stood between
them.]]]

13 [(M) Begun long years ago, their friendship had
petered out on a Westmoreland road, [(A-1) where
the hen spread her wings before her chicks;]] [(M)
after which Ramsay had married,] and [(M) their
paths lying different ways there had been, certainly
for no one's fault, some tendency, [(Av-1) when they
met,] to repeat.]

(pp. 133–5)

14 [(M) [(N-1) 'People soon drift apart,'] said Mr
Bankes, feeling, however, some satisfaction [(Av-1)
when he thought [(N-2) that after all he knew both
the Mannings and the Ramsays.]]]

15 [(M) [(N-1) He had not drifted apart] he thought,].
~~laying down his spoon and wiping his clean shaven~~
~~lips punctiliously.~~

16 [(M) [(N-1) But perhaps he was rather unusual, he
thought, in this; [(N-2) he never let himself get into
a groove.]]]

17 [(M) He had friends in all circles.] . . . ~~Mrs Ramsay~~
~~had to break off here to tell the maid something~~
~~about keeping the food hot.~~

18 [(M) That was [(N-1) why he preferred dining
alone.]]

19 [(M) All those interruptions annoyed him.]

20 [(M) [(N-1) Well, thought William Bankes, ~~preserving~~
~~a demeanour of exquisite courtesy and merely~~
~~spreading the fingers of his left hand on the tablecloth~~
~~as a mechanic examines a tool beautifully polished~~
~~and ready for use in an interval of leisure~~, such are
the sacrifices [(A-2) one's friends ask one.]]]

21 [(M) It would have hurt her [(Av-1) if he had refused to come.]]

22 [(M) But it was not worth it for him.]

23 ~~Looking at his hand,~~ [(M) he thought [(N-1) that
[(Av-2) if he had been alone] dinner would have
been almost over now;] [(N-1) he would have been
free to work.]]

24 [(M) Yes, he thought, [(N-1) it is a terrible waste of
time.]]

25 [(M) The children were dropping in still.] 'I ~~wish~~
~~one . . .' Mrs Ramsay was saying.~~

26 [(M) [(N-1) How trifling it all is,] [(N-1) how boring
it all is, he thought, compared with the other thing
—work.]] . . .

27 [(M) What a waste of time it all was to be sure!]
28 [(M) [(N-1) Yet, he thought, she is one of my oldest friends.]]
29 [(M) I am by way of being devoted to her.]
30 [(M) Yet now, at this moment her presence meant absolutely nothing to him;] [(M) her beauty meant nothing to him;] her sitting with her little boy at the window—nothing, nothing.
31 [(M) He wished only to be alone and to take up that book.]
32 ~~He felt uncomfortable~~; [(M) he felt treacherous, [(Av-1) that he could sit by her side and feel nothing for her.]]
33 [(M) The truth was [(N-1) that he did not enjoy family life.]]
34 [(M) It was in this sort of state [(A-1) that one asked oneself, [(N-2) What does one live for?]]]
35 [(M) [(N-1) Why, one asked oneself, does one take all these pains for the human race to go on?]]
36 [(M) Is it so very desirable?]
37 [(M) Are we attractive as a species?]
38 [(M) Not so very, he thought,] ~~looking at those rather untidy boys.~~
39 [(M) [(N-1) His favourite, Cam, was in bed,] he supposed.]
40 Foolish questions, vain questions, questions [(A-1) one never asked [(Av-2) if one was occupied.]]
41 [(M) Is human life this?]
42 [(M) Is human life that?]
43 [(M) One never had time to think about it.]
44 [(M) But here he was asking himself that sort of question, [(Av-1) because Mrs Ramsay was giving orders to servants,] and also [(Av-1) because it had struck him, thinking [(N-2) how surprised Mrs Ramsay was [(Av-3) that Carrie Manning should still exist,]] [(N-2) that friendships, even the best of them, are frail things.]]]
45 [(M) One drifts apart.] . . .

46 [(M) He was sitting beside Mrs Ramsay] and [(M) he had nothing in the world to say to her.]

(p. 141)

47 ... [(M) Conscious of his treachery, conscious of her wish to talk about something more intimate, yet out of mood for it at present, he felt come over him the disagreeableness of life, sitting there, waiting.]

48 [(M) Perhaps the others were saying something interesting?]

49 [(M) What were they saying?]

50 [(N-1) That the fishing season was bad;] [(N-1) that the men were emigrating.]

51 [(M) They were talking about wages and unemployment.]

52 [(M) The young man was abusing the government.]

53 [(M) William Bankes, thinking [(N-1) what a relief it* was to catch on to something of this sort [(Av-2) when private life was disagreeable,]] heard him say something about] ~~'one of the most scandalous acts of the present government.'~~

* 840 words.

Charles Tansley

(p. 20)

1 [(M) He would like her to see him, gowned and hooded, walking in a procession.]

2 [(M) A fellowship, a professorship, he felt capable of anything and saw himself]—but [(M) what was she looking at?]

3 At a man pasting a bill.

(pp. 21–2)

4 [(M) It was a large family, nine brothers and sisters,] and [(M) his father was a working man.]

5 [(M) 'My father is a chemist, Mrs Ramsay.]

6 [(M) He keeps a shop.']

7 [(M) He himself had paid his own way [(Av-1) since
   he was thirteen.]]

8 [(M) Often he went without a greatcoat in winter.]

9 [(M) He could never 'return hospitality' (~~those were
   his parched stiff words~~) at college.]

10 [(M) He had to make things last twice the time [(A-1)
   other people did;]] [(M) he smoked the cheapest
   tobacco;] shag; the same [(A-1) the old men did in
   the quays.]

11 [(M) He worked hard—seven hours a day;]

(pp. 24–5)

12 [(M) He heard her quick step above; heard her voice
   cheerful, then low; looked at the mats, tea-caddies,
   glass shades; waited quite impatiently; looked forward eagerly to the walk home; determined to carry
   her bag; then heard her come out; shut a door; say
   [(N-1) they must keep the windows open and the
   doors shut, ask at the house for anything [(A-2) they
   wanted] [(P-2) (she must be talking to a child)]]
   [(Av-1) when, suddenly, in she came, stood for a
   moment silent [(P-2) (as if she had been pretending
   up there, and for a moment let herself be now),]
   stood quite motionless for a moment against a picture of Queen Victoria wearing the blue ribbon of
   the Garter;] [(Av-1) when all at once he realized
   [(N-2) that it was this:] [(N-2) it was this:]—[(N-2)
   she was the most beautiful person [(A-3) he had
   ever seen.]]]]]

13 [(M) With stars in her eyes and veils in her hair, with
   cyclamen and wild violets—what nonsense was he
   thinking?]

14 [(M) She was fifty at least;] [(M) she had eight
   children.]

15 Stepping through fields of flowers and taking to her
   breast buds [(A-1) that had broken] and lambs
   [(A-1) that had fallen;] with the stars in her eyes and
   the wind in her hair—~~he took her bag.~~

(pp. 129–30)

16 [(M) [(N-1) He wrote to his mother;] [(N-1) otherwise he did not suppose [(N-2) he wrote one letter a month,]] said Mr Tansley, ~~shortly~~.]

17 [(M) For he was not going to talk the sort of rot [(A-1) these people wanted him to talk.]]

18 [(M) He was not going to be condescended to by these silly women.]

19 [(M) He had been reading in his room,] and [(M) now he came down] and [(M) it all seemed to him silly, superficial, flimsy.]

20 [(M) Why did they dress?]

21 [(M) He had come down in his ordinary clothes.]

22 [(M) He had not got any dress clothes.]

23 [(M) [(N-1) 'One never gets anything worth having by post']—that was the sort of thing [(A-1) they were always saying.]]

24 [(M) They made men say that sort of thing.]

25 [(M) [(N-1) Yes, it was pretty well true,] he thought.]

26 [(M) They never got anything worth having from one year's end to another.]

27 [(M) They did nothing but talk, talk, talk, eat, eat, eat.]

28 [(M) It was the women's fault.]

29 [(M) Women made civilization impossible with all their 'charm', with all their silliness.]

30 [(M) 'No going to the Lighthouse tomorrow, Mrs Ramsay,' he said, ~~asserting himself~~.]

31 [(M) He liked her;] [(M) he admired her;] [(M) he still thought of the man in the drain-pipe looking up at her;] [(M) but he felt it necessary to assert himself.] . . .

(pp. 130–1)

32 [(M) [(N-1) She was telling lies] he could see.]

33 [(M) She was saying [(N-1) what she did not mean] to annoy him, for some reason.]

34 [(M) She was laughing at him.]

35 [(M) He was in his old flannel trousers.]

36 [(M) He had no others.]

37 [(M) He felt very rough and isolated and lonely.]

38 [(M) He knew [(N-1) that she was trying to tease him for some reason;] [(N-1) she didn't want to go to the Lighthouse with him;] [(N-1) she despised him;] [(N-1) so did Prue Ramsay;] [(N-1) so did they all.]]

39 [(M) But he was not going to be made a fool of by women, ~~so he turned deliberately in his chair and looked out of the window and said, all in a jerk, very rudely,~~ [(N-1) it would be too rough for her to-morrow.]]

40 [(M) She would be sick.]

41 [(M) It annoyed him [(N-1) that she should have made him speak like that, with Mrs Ramsay listening.]]

42 [(M) [(N-1) If only he could be alone in his room working, he thought, among his books.]]

43 [(M) That was [(N-1) where he felt at his ease.]]

44 [(M) And he had never run a penny into debt;] [(M) he had never cost his father a penny [(Av-1) since he was fifteen;]] [(M) he had helped them at home out of his savings;] [(M) he was educating his sister.]

45 [(M) Still, he wished [(N-1) he had known how to answer Miss Briscoe properly;]] [(M) he wished [(N-1) it had not come out all in a jerk like that.]]

46 [(M) 'You'd be sick.']

47 [(M) He wished [(N-1) he could think of something to say to Mrs Ramsay, something [(A-2) which would show her [(N-3) that he was not just a dry prig.]]]]

48 [(M) That was [(N-1) what they all thought him.]]

49 [(M) [(N-1) They did talk nonsense, he thought, the Ramsays;]] ~~and he pounced on this fresh instance with joy, making a note which,~~ [(N-1) one of these days, he would read aloud to one or two friends.]

50 [(M) There, in a society [(A-1) where one could say

[(N-2) what one liked]] he would sarcastically describe 'staying with the Ramsays' and [(N-1) what nonsense they talked.]]

51 [(M) [(N-1) It was worth while doing it once, he would say; but not again.]]

52 [(M) [(N-1) The women bored one so,] he would say.]

53 [(M) Of course Ramsay had dished himself by marrying a beautiful woman and having eight children.]

Lily Briscoe
(pp. 75-8)

1 . . . [(M) she felt herself praised.]

2 [(M) Let him gaze;] [(M) she would steal a look at her picture.]

3 [(M) She could have wept.]

4 [(M) It was bad,] [(M) it was bad,] [(M) it was infinitely bad!]

5 [(M) She could have done it differently of course;] [(M) the colour could have been thinned and faded;] the shapes etherealized; [(M) that was [(N-1) how Paunceforte would have seen it.]]

6 [(M) But then she did not see it like that.]

7 [(M) She saw the colour burning on a framework of steel; the light of a butterfly's wing lying upon the arches of a cathedral.]

8 [(M) Of all that only a few random marks scrawled upon the canvas remained.]

9 [(M) And it would never be seen; never be hung even,] and [(M) there was Mr Tansley whispering in her ear,] 'Women can't paint, women can't write . . .'

10 [(M) She now remembered [(N-1) what she had been going to say about Mrs Ramsay.]]

11 [(M) She did not know [(N-1) how she would have put it;]] [(M) but it would have been something critical.]

12 [(M) She had been annoyed the other night by some highhandedness.]

13 ~~Looking along the level of Mr Bankes's glance at her,~~
[(M) she thought [(N-1) that no woman could worship another woman in the way [(A-2) he worshipped;]] [(N-1) they could only seek shelter under
the shade [(A-2) which Mr Bankes extended over
them both.]]]

14 ~~Looking along his beam, she added to it her different
ray,~~ thinking [(N-1) that she was unquestionably the
loveliest of people (bowed over her book); the best
perhaps; but also, different too from the perfect
shape [(A-2) which one saw there.]]

15 [(M) But why different, and how different? she asked
herself, ~~scraping her palette of all those mounds of
blue and green~~ [(A-1) which seemed to her like clods
with no life in them now,]] [(M) yet she vowed,
[(N-1) she would inspire them, force them to move,
flow, do her bidding tomorrow.]]

16 [(M) How did she differ?]

17 [(M) What was the spirit in her, the essential thing,
[(A-1) by which, [(Av-2) had you found a crumpled
glove in the corner of a sofa,] you would have known
it, from its twisted finger, hers indisputably?]]

18 [(M) She was like a bird for speed, an arrow for
directness.]

19 [(M) She was wilful;] [(M) she was commanding (of
course, [(P-1) Lily reminded herself, [(N-2) I am
thinking of her relations with women,] and [(N-2) I
am much younger, an insignificant person, living off
the Brompton Road]]).]

20 [(M) She opened bedroom windows.]

21 [(M) She shut doors.] . . .

22 [(M) Arriving late at night, with a light tap on one's
bedroom door, wrapped in an old fur coat [(P-1) (for
the setting of her beauty was always that—hasty, but
apt),] she would enact again [(N-1) whatever it
might be—Charles Tansley losing his umbrella;
Mr Carmichael snuffling and sniffing; Mr Bankes
saying, '~~The vegetable salts are lost.~~']]

23 [(M) All this she would adroitly shape; even maliciously twist; and, moving over to the window, in pretence [(A-1) that she must go,] [(P-1) —it was dawn,] [(P-1) she could see the sun rising,] —half turn back, more intimately, but still always laughing, insist [(N-1) that she must, Minta must, they all must marry, [(Av-2) since in the whole world [(Av-3) whatever laurels might be tossed to her [(P-4) (but Mrs Ramsay cared not a fig for her painting),] or triumphs won by her [(P-4) (probably Mrs Ramsay had had her share of those),]] [(P-3) and here she saddened, darkened, and came back to her chair,] there could be no disputing this: [(N-3) an unmarried woman [(P-4) (she lightly took her hand for a moment),] an unmarried woman has missed the best of life.]]]]

24 [(M) The house seemed full of children sleeping and Mrs Ramsay listening; shaded lights and regular breathing.]

25 [(M) [(N-1) Oh, but, Lily would say, there was her father; her home; even, [(Av-2) had she dared to say it,] her painting.]]

26 [(M) But all this seemed so little, so virginal, against the other.]

27 [(M) Yet, [(Av-1) as the night wore on, and white lights parted the curtains, and even now and then some bird chirped in the garden,] gathering a desperate courage she would urge her own exemption from the universal law; plead for it;] [(M) she liked to be alone;] [(M) she liked to be herself;] [(M) she was not made for that; and so have to meet a serious stare from eyes of unparalleled depth, and confront Mrs Ramsay's simple certainty [(P-1) (and she was childlike now)] [(A-1) that her dear Lily, her little Brisk, was a fool.]]

28 [(M) [(N-1) Then, she remembered, she had laid her head on Mrs Ramsay's lap and laughed and laughed and laughed, laughed almost hysterically at the

thought of Mrs Ramsay presiding with immutable calm over destinies [(A-2) which she completely failed to understand.]]]

29 [(M) There she sat, simple, serious.]

30 [(M) She had recovered her sense of her now— [(N-1) this was the glove's twisted finger.]]

31 [(M) But into what sanctuary had one penetrated?]

32 [(M) Lily Briscoe had looked up at last,] and [(M) there was Mrs Ramsay, unwitting entirely [(N-1) what had caused her laughter,] still presiding, but now with every trace of wilfulness abolished, and in its stead, something clear as the space [(A-1) which the clouds at last uncover]—the little space of sky [(A-1) which sleeps beside the moon.]]

33 [(M) Was it wisdom?]

34 [(M) Was it knowledge?]

35 [(M) Was it, once more, the deceptiveness of beauty, [(Av-1) so that all one's perceptions, half way to truth, were tangled in a golden mesh?]] or [(M) did she lock up within her some secret [(A-1) which certainly Lily Briscoe believed [(N-2) people must have for the world to go on at all?]]]

36 [(M) Every one could not be as helter skelter, hand to mouth [(Av-1) as she was.]] But* if they knew, could they tell one what they knew?

* 840 words.

Mrs McNab

(pp. 203–5)

1 Thinking no harm, [(Av-1) for the family would not come, never again, [(P-2) some said,] and the house would be sold at Michaelmas perhaps,] ~~Mrs McNab stooped and picked a bunch of flowers to take home with her. She laid them on the table while she dusted.~~

2 [(M) She was fond of flowers.]

3 [(M) It was a pity to let them waste.]

4 [(M) [(Av-1) Suppose the house were sold] (~~she stood
arms akimbo in front of the looking glass~~) it would
want seeing to]—[(M) it would.]

5 [(M) There it had stood all these years without a soul
in it.]

6 [(M) The books and things were mouldy, [(Av-1) for,
what with the war and help being hard to get, the
house had not been cleaned [(Av-2) as she could have
wished.]]]

7 [(M) It was beyond one person's strength to get it
straight now.]

8 [(M) She was too old.]

9 [(M) Her legs pained her.]

10 [(M) All those books needed to be laid out on the grass
in the sun;] [(M) there was plaster fallen in the hall;]
[(M) the rain-pipe had blocked over the study window and let the water in;] [(M) the carpet was
ruined quite.]

11 [(M) But people should come themselves;] [(M) they
should have sent somebody down to see.]

12 [(M) For there were clothes in the cupboards;] [(M)
they had left clothes in all the bedrooms.]

13 [(M) What was she to do with them?]

14 [(M) They had the moth in them—Mrs Ramsay's
things.]

15 Poor lady!

16 [(M) She would never want *them* again.]

17 [(M) [(N-1) She was dead,] they said;] years ago in
London.

18 [(M) There was the old grey cloak [(A-1) she wore
gardening]] (~~Mrs McNab fingered it~~).

19 [(M) She could see her, [(Av-1) as she came up the
drive with the washing, stooping over her flowers]
[(P-1) (the garden was a pitiful sight now, all run to
riot, and rabbits scuttling at you out of the beds)]] —
[(M) she could see her with one of the children by
her in that grey cloak.]

20 [(M) There were boots and shoes; and a brush and

comb left on the dressing-table, for all the world [(Av-1) as if she expected to come back tomorrow.]]

21 [(M) [(N-1) (She had died very sudden at the end,] they said.)]

22 [(M) And once they had been coming, but had put off coming, what with the war, and travel being so difficult these days;] [(M) they had never come all these years; just sent her money; but never wrote, never came, and expected to find things [(Av-1) as they had left them,] ah, dear!]

23 [(M) Why the dressing-table drawers were full of things (she pulled them open), handkerchiefs, bits of ribbon.]

24 [(M) Yes, she could see Mrs Ramsay [(Av-1) as she came up the drive with the washing.]]

25 'Good evening, Mrs McNab,' [(M) she would say.]

26 [(M) She had a pleasant way with her.]

27 [(M) The girls all liked her.]

28 [(M) But, dear, many things had changed since then] (she shut the drawer); [(M) many families had lost their dearest.]

29 [(M) So she was dead; and Mr Andrew killed; and Miss Prue dead too, [(P-1) they said,] with her first baby;] [(M) but every one had lost some one these years.]

30 [(M) Prices had gone up shamefully, and didn't come down again neither.]

31 [(M) She could well remember her in her grey cloak.]

32 'Good evening, Mrs McNab,' [(M) she said, and told cook to keep a plate of milk soup for her — quite thought [(N-1) she wanted it,] carrying that heavy basket all the way up from town.]

33 [(M) She could see her now stooping over her flowers.]

(p. 206)

34 And cook's name now?

35 Mildred?

36 Marian? — some name like that.

37 [(M) Ah, she had forgotten] [(M)—she did forget things.]

38 Fiery, like all red-haired women.

39 [(M) Many a laugh they had had.]

40 [(M) She was always welcome in the kitchen.]

41 [(M) She made them laugh,] [(M) she did.]

42 [(M) Things were better then than now.]

43 . . . [(M) there was too much work for one woman.] ~~She wagged her head this side and that.~~

44 [(M) This had been the nursery.]

45 [(M) Why, it was all damp in here;] [(M) the plaster was falling.]

46 [(M) Whatever did they want to hang a beast's skull there?] gone mouldy too.

47 And rats in all the attics.

48 [(M) The rain came in.]

49 [(M) But they never sent; never came.]

50 [(M) Some of the locks had gone, [(Av-1) so the doors banged.]]

51 [(M) She didn't like to be up here at dusk alone neither.]

52 [(M) It was too much for one woman, too much, too much.]

(pp. 210–11)

53 ~~Once more, as she felt the warm tea in her, the telescope fitted itself to Mrs. McNab's eyes, and in a ring of light~~ [(M) she saw the old gentleman, lean as a rake, wagging his head, [(Av-1) as she came up with the washing, talking to himself, [(P-2) she supposed,]] on the lawn.]

54 [(M) He never noticed her.]

55 [(M) Some said [(N-1) he was dead;]] [(M) some said [(N-1) she was dead.]]

56 [(M) Which was it?]

57 [(M) Mrs Bast didn't know for certain either.]

58 [(M) The young gentleman was dead.]

59 [(M) That she was sure.]

60 [(M) She had read his name in the papers.]

61 [(M) There was the cook now, Mildred, Marian, some such name as that—a red-headed woman, quick-tempered like all her sort, but kind, too, [(Av-1) if you knew the way with her.]]

62 [(M) Many a laugh they had had together.]

63 [(M) She saved a plate of soup for Maggie; a bite of ham, sometimes; [(N-1) whatever was over.]]

64 [(M) They lived well in those days.]

65 [(M) They had everything [(A-1) they wanted]] (~~glibly, jovially, with the tea hot in her she unwound her ball of memories, sitting in the wicker arm chair by the nursery fender~~).

66 [(M) There was always plenty doing, people in the house, twenty staying sometimes, and washing up till long past midnight.] . . .

67 [(M) [(N-1) It might well be,] said Mrs McNab,] ~~wantoning on with her memories~~; [(M) they had friends in eastern countries; gentlemen staying there, ladies in evening dress;] [(M) she had seen them once through the dining-room door all sitting at dinner.]

68 Twenty [(M-1) she dared say] in all their jewellery, and she asked to stay help wash up, might be till after midnight.

APPENDIX B

Stylistic Analysis Statistics

As the sampling procedure described in Chapter Two suggests, these are not strictly random samples. However, there is no reason to suspect any bias in sampling; that is, that samples from different sections of the novel would yield data different from these. But that is an untested assumption. The probability (p) values,* therefore, should be taken as indications of the magnitudes of differences—including relative magnitudes—rather than as strict probability levels.

Presented in the following tables are the significance levels of Chi-Square at p = ·05 and at p = ·01. The results show that of the 39 variables 51% were significant at ·05 and that 38% were significant at ·01.

* Acknowledgement is tendered to the Academic Computing Centre at New York University where these statistical computations were performed and to the statistical consultant, Patricia Waly.

Table 1

SENTENCE STRUCTURE*

Measure	Mrs Ramsay	Mr Ramsay	James Ramsay	Cam Ramsay	Omniscient Narrator	William Bankes	Charles Tansley	Lily Briscoe	Mrs McNab	Chi-Square
No. Sentences	58·	36·	40·	40·	30·	53·	53·	36·	68·	27·26‡
No. Fragments	4·	4·	2·	1·	1·	3·	3·	2·	8·	11·86
No. Clauses	103·	82·	99·	106·	76·	108·	111·	92·	101·	11·71
No. Main Clauses	65·	46·	57·	51·	40·	59·	64·	48·	76·	17·78†
No. Adverbial Clauses	14·	17·	10·	12·	10·	12·	4·	7·	11·	10·54
No. Adjectival Clauses	7·	11·	11·	6·	8·	7·	10·	11·	2·	8·99
No. Noun Clauses	16·	8·	17·	33·	16·	32·	31·	17·	7·	40·48‡
No. Parenthetical Clauses	2·	1·	5·	5·	3·	3·	3·	10·	6·	13·63

Distribution of Embedded Clause Types	61·62‡
Ratio: Main Clauses/Embedded Clauses	23·64‡

† p = ·05 for 8 df: 15·51   ‡ p = ·01 for 8 df: 20·09

Table 2

LATINATE AND CONTENT WORDS

Measure	Mrs Ramsay	Mr Ramsay	James Ramsay	Cam Ramsay	Omniscient Narrator	William Bankes	Charles Tansley	Lily Briscoe	Mrs McNab	Chi-Square
No. Nouns with Latin Suffixes	10·	23·	9·	5·	15·	29·	4·	9·	4·	51·50‡
No. Latin Derived Verbs	7·	11·	12·	10·	27·	21·	12·	19·	7·	26·71‡
% Content Words	34·	35·	36·	37·	56·	36·	34·	39·	36·	9·94

‡ p = ·01 for 8 df: 20·09.

* Unless otherwise indicated, Chi-Square is computed for frequency of occurrence in total sample of 840 words per narrator.

Table 3
VERBALS AND FINITE VERBS

Measure	Mrs Ramsay	Mr Ramsay	James Ramsay	Cam Ramsay	Omniscient Narrator	William Bankes	Charles Tansley	Lily Briscoe	Mrs McNab	Chi-Square
No. Participles	17·	22·	20·	27·	37·	23·	14·	30·	19·	17·38†
No. Gerunds	8·	3·	4·	2·	1·	2·	3·	2·	2·	11·33
No. Infinitives	19·	13·	11·	12·	2·	14·	20·	11·	17·	17·51†
Distribution of Types of Verbals										42·34‡
No. Verbals	44·	38·	35·	41·	40·	38·	37·	43·	38·	1·73
No. Finite Verbs	114·	90·	109·	113·	109·	112·	128·	114·	114·	6·89
Ratio: Verbals/Finite Verbs										2·82
No. Transitive Verbs	52·	50·	52·	60·	48·	56·	70·	51·	56·	6·55
No. Intransitive Verbs	60·	40·	57·	53·	61·	56·	58·	63·	58·	6·47
Ratio: Transitive Verbs/Intransitive Verbs										5·96
No. 'Action' Verbs	11·	11·	32·	34·	43·	10·	12·	15·	15·	61·18‡
No. Cognitive Verbs	10·	4·	13·	15·	1·	22·	17·	10·	11·	28·51‡
No. Copulative Verbs	37·	15·	21·	24·	17·	37·	24·	29·	30·	19·31†

† p = ·05 for 8 df: 15·51. ‡ p = ·01 for 8 df: 20·09.

Table 4
NOUNS AND PRONOUNS

Measure	Mrs Ramsay	Mr Ramsay	James Ramsay	Cam Ramsay	Omniscient Narrator	William Bankes	Charles Tansley	Lily Briscoe	Mrs McNab	Chi-Square
No. Nouns	138·	160·	142·	135·	184·	161·	136·	152·	153·	13·26
No. Common Nouns	130·	139·	131·	123·	180·	130·	119·	126·	140·	19·30†
No. Proper Nouns	8·	21·	11·	12·	4·	31·	17·	26·	13·	38·32‡
No. Abstract Nouns	50·	72·	24·	16·	36·	74·	30·	45·	19·	90·74‡
No. Pronouns	121·	91·	95·	116·	63·	106·	138·	103·	110·	33·93‡
No. Personal Pronouns	99·	64·	65·	90·	40·	74·	112·	75·	89·	46·93‡
No. Demonstrative Pronouns	6·	3·	8·	5·	2·	7·	7·	7·	4·	6·28
No. Indefinite Pronouns	8·	6·	16·	7·	11·	13·	8·	4·	9·	11·95

† p = ·05 for 8 df: 15·51. ‡ p = ·01 for 8 df: 20·09.

Table 5
UNGROUPED VARIABLES

Measure	Mrs Ramsay	Mr Ramsay	James Ramsay	Cam Ramsay	Omniscient Narrator	William Bankes	Charles Tansley	Lily Briscoe	Mrs McNab	Chi-Square
No. Syllables	1109·	1112·	1069·	1078·	1148·	1138·	1082·	1157·	1035·	11·90
No. Articles	38·	69·	68·	66·	89·	43·	49·	55·	57·	32·80‡
No. Indefinite Articles	15·	11·	24·	25·	14·	14·	25·	20·	13·	14·14
No. Descriptive Adjectives	50·	37·	45·	43·	49·	47·	36·	45·	43·	4·26
No. Unmodified Common Nouns preceded by 'the'	18·	39·	26·	33·	52·	22·	13·	27·	36·	38·24‡

‡ p = ·01 for 8 df: 20·09.

To the Lighthouse
(Entire Novel)

Narrators	No. Lines	Per cent
Lily Briscoe	2087·0	27·3
Mrs Ramsay	1949·5	25·5
Omniscient	1507·0	19·7
Mr Ramsay	495·0	6·5
William Bankes	295·0	3·9
Cam Ramsay	256·0	3·3
James Ramsay	241·5	3·2
Charles Tansley	168·5	2·2
Mrs McNab	102·5	1·3
James and Cam	94·5	1·2
Paul Rayley	55·0	0·7
Nancy Ramsay	53·0	0·7
Andrew Ramsay	40·5	0·5
Minta Doyle	34·0	0·4
Prue Ramsay	19·5	0·3
Other	19·0	0·3
Mrs Bast	16·0	0·2
Jasper Ramsay	10·5	0·1
(Indeterminable	210·0	2·7)

APPENDIX B

To the Lighthouse
('The Window')

Narrators	No. Lines	Per cent
Mrs Ramsay	1939·5	42·0
Omniscient	778·5	17·0
Lily Briscoe	587·5	13·0
Mr Ramsay	370·0	8·0
William Bankes	293·0	6·0
Charles Tansley	168·5	4·0
Other	156·0	4·0
Paul Rayley	55·0	1·0
Nancy Ramsay	53·0	1·0
(Indeterminable	170·0	4·0)

('Time Passes')

Omniscient	492·0	76·0
Mrs McNab	102·5	16·0
Lily Briscoe	16·5	3·0
Mrs Bast	16·0	2·0
Other	9·0	1·0
(Indeterminable	14·0	2·0)

('The Lighthouse')

Lily Briscoe	1483·0	61·0
Cam Ramsay	256·0	11·0
Omniscient	236·5	10·0
James Ramsay	199·0	8·0
Mr Ramsay	125·0	5·0
James and Cam	94·5	4·0
Other	3·0	0·1
(Indeterminable	26·0	0·9)

BIBLIOGRAPHY

Abrams, M. H. The Mirror and the Lamp: Romantic
Theory and the Critical Tradition. New York, W. W.
Norton and Company, Inc., 1953.

Allport, Gordon W. Personality. New York, Henry Holt
and Company, 1937.

Alonzo, Amado. 'The Stylistic Interpretation of Literary
Texts', *Modern Language Notes*, LVII (1942), 489–96.

Ames, Van Meter. Aesthetics of the Novel. Chicago,
University of Chicago Press, 1928.

Auerbach, Erich. Mimesis: The Representation of Reality
in Western Literature. Translated by Willard Trask.
Garden City, New York, Doubleday Anchor Books,
1953.

Beach, Joseph Warren. The Twentieth Century Novel:
Studies in Technique. New York and London, D.
Appleton-Century Company, 1932.

Beckson, Karl, and Arthur Ganz. A Reader's Guide to
Literary Terms, New York, Farrar, Straus and Cudahy,
1960.

Bennett, Joan. Virginia Woolf: Her Art as a Novelist.
2nd ed. revised. Cambridge, Cambridge University
Press, 1964.

Bentley, Phyllis. Some Observations on the Art of Narrative. New York, The Macmillan Company, 1947.

Berelson, Bernard. 'Content Analysis', *Handbook in Social
Psychology*, ed. Gardner Lindzey. Cambridge, Mass.,
Addison-Wesley Publishing Co., Inc., 1954, pp. 488–
522.

Bevis, Dorothy. '*The Waves*: A Fusion of Symbol, Style and
Thought in Virginia Woolf', *Twentieth-Century Literature*
II (1956), 5–20.

Blackall, Jean Frantz. Jamesian Ambiguity and *The Sacred
Fount*. Ithaca, Cornell University Press, 1965.

Blackmur, Richard P. Language as Gesture. New York, Harcourt, Brace and Company, Inc., 1952.

Blackstone, Bernard. Virginia Woolf: A Commentary. London, The Hogarth Press, 1949.

Booth, Wayne C. The Rhetoric of Fiction. Chicago, University of Chicago Press, 1961.

——'The Self-Conscious Narrator in Comic Fiction before Tristram Shandy', PMLA, LXVII (1952), 163–85.

Borroff, Marie. Sir Gawain and the Green Knight: A Stylistic and Metrical Study. New York and London, Yale University Press, 1962.

Bowling, Lawrence E. 'What is the Stream of Consciousness Technique?', PMLA, LXV (1950), 333–45.

Bradbrook, M. C. 'Notes on the Style of Mrs Woolf', Scrutiny, I (May, 1932), 33–8.

Brown, E. K. Rhythm in the Novel. Toronto, University of Toronto Press, 1950.

Brown, Roger. Words and Things. Glencoe, Illinois, Free Press, 1958.

Burke, Kenneth. A Rhetoric of Motives. New York, Prentice-Hall, 1950.

Chambers, R. L. The Novels of Virginia Woolf. Edinburgh, Oliver and Boyd, 1947.

Chomsky, Noam A. Syntactic Structures. 's-Gravenhage, Mouton, 1957.

Church, Margaret. Time and Reality: Studies in Contemporary Fiction. Chapel Hill, University of North Carolina Press, 1963.

Comfort, Alex. The Novel and Our Time. London, Phoenix House, 1948.

Daiches, David. Virginia Woolf. Norfolk, Conn., New Directions Books, 1942.

Delattre, Floris. Le Roman psychologique de Virginia Woolf. Paris, J. Vrin, 1932.

Derbyshire, S. H. 'An Analysis of Mrs Woolf's To the Lighthouse', College English, III (January, 1942), 353–360.

DeVoto, Bernard. 'The Invisible Novelist', The World

of Fiction. Boston, Houghton Mifflin Company, 1950, pp. 205-25.

Dobrée, Bonamy. Modern Prose Style. Oxford, Oxford University Press, 1934.

Doner, Dean. 'Virginia Woolf: The Service of Style', *Modern Fiction Studies*, II (1956), 1-12.

Drew, Elizabeth. The Novel: A Modern Guide to Fifteen English Masterpieces. New York, W. W. Norton and Company, Inc., 1963.

Edel, Leon. The Modern Psychological Novel. New York, Grove Press, Inc., 1959.

Empson, William. Seven Types of Ambiguity. New York, Meridian Books, Inc., 1955.

Fernandez, Roman. Messages. Translated by Montgomery Belgion. Paris, Librarie Gallimard, 1926.

Forster, E. M. Aspects of the Novel. New York, Harcourt, Brace and Company, Inc., 1927.

Francis, W. Nelson. The Structure of American English. New York, The Ronald Press Company, 1958.

Freedman, Ralph. The Lyrical Novel: Studies in Hermann Hesse, André Gide, and Virginia Woolf. Princeton, Princeton University Press, 1963.

Friedman, Melvin J. Stream of Consciousness: A Study in Literary Method. New Haven, Yale Univ. Press, 1955.

Friedman, Norman. 'Point of View in Fiction: The Development of a Critical Concept', *PMLA*, LXX (December, 1955), 1160-84.

——'The Waters of Annihilation: Double Vision in *To the Lighthouse*', *Journal of English Literary History*, XXII (1955), 61-79.

Fries, Charles C. The Structure of English. New York, Harcourt, Brace and Company, Inc., 1952.

Frohock, W. M. 'Camus: Image, Influence and Sensibility', *Yale French Studies*, II (1949), 91-9.

Frye, Northrop. Anatomy of Criticism. Princeton, Princeton University Press, 1957.

Gerould, Gordon Hall. How to Read Fiction. Princeton, Princeton University Press, 1937.

Goodman, Paul. The Structure of Literature. Chicago and London, University of Chicago Press, 1954.

Gordon, Caroline. 'Some Readings and Misreadings', *Sewanee Review*, LXI (1953), 384–407.

Hafley, James. The Glass Roof: Virginia Woolf as Novelist. Berkeley and Los Angeles, University of California Press, 1954.

Harris, Zellig S. Methods in Structural Linguistics. Chicago, University of Chicago Press, 1951.

Hasley, Louis. 'The Stream-of-Consciousness Method', *Catholic World*, CXLVI (1937), 210–13.

Hatcher, Anna G. 'Syntax and the Sentence', *Word*, XII (1956), 234–50.

Hayakawa, S. I. Language in Thought and Action. New York, Harcourt, Brace and World, Inc., 1949.

Heath, Louise R. The Concept of Time. Chicago, University of Chicago Press, 1936.

Higashida, Chiaki. 'On the Prose Style of D. H. Lawrence', *Studies in English Literature* (Tokyo University), XIX (1939), 545–6.

Hoffmann, Charles G. 'Virginia Woolf's *To the Lighthouse*', *Explicator* (November, 1951), Item 13.

Humphrey, Robert. Stream of Consciousness in the Modern Novel. Berkeley and Los Angeles, University of California Press, 1954.

——' "Stream of Consciousness": Technique or Genre?', *Philological Quarterly*, XXX (1951), 434–7.

James, Henry. The Art of Fiction and Other Essays, ed. M. Roberts. New York, Oxford University Press, 1948.

——The Art of the Novel: Critical Prefaces. New York, Charles Scribner's Sons, 1934.

Jenkins, J. J., and W. A. Russell. 'Associative Clustering During Recall', *Journal of Abnormal and Social Psychology*, 47 (1952), 818–21.

Jespersen, Otto. The Philosophy of Grammar. London, G. Allen and Unwin, Ltd., 1935.

Kamiya, Miyeko. 'Virginia Woolf: An Outline of a Study on her Personality, Illness, and Work', *Confinia Psychiatrica*

(Tsuda College, Kodaira, Tokyo), VIII (1965), 189–205.

Korzybski, Alfred. Science and Sanity: An Introduction to Non-Aristotelean Systems and General Semantics. Lakeville, Conn., International Non-Aristotelean Library Publishing Company, 1948.

Lambek, J. 'Mathematics of Sentence Structure', *American Mathematical Monthly*, 65 (1958), 154–70.

Lambert, Mildred. 'Studies in Stylistics', *American Speech*, III (1929), 173–81, 326–33; IV (1929), 28–39, 137–44, 228–43, 395–402, 477–89.

Langer, Susanne K. Feeling and Form. New York, Charles Scribner's Sons, 1953.

——Philosophy in a New Key: A Study in the Symbolism of Reason, Rite, and Art. 2nd ed., Cambridge, Mass., Harvard University Press, 1957.

Lee, Vernon [Violet Paget]. The Handling of Words, and Other Studies in Literary Psychology. New York, Dodd, Mead and Company, 1923.

Lees, Robert B. The Grammar of English Nominalizations. Bloomington, Publication No. 12 of Indiana University Research Center in anthropology, folklore, and linguistics, 1960.

Lever, Katherine. The Novel and the Reader. London, Methuen and Company, Ltd., 1961.

Lubbock, Percy. The Craft of Fiction. London, Jonathan Cape, Ltd., 1921.

Lucas, F. L. Style. London, Cassell, 1955.

Lynch, J. J. 'The Tonality of Lyric Poetry: An Experiment in Method', *Word*, IX (1953), 211–24.

Mann, M. B. 'Studies in Language Behavior', *Psychological Monographs*, 56 (1944), 41–74.

Martin, Harold C., ed. Style in Prose Fiction; English Institute Essays, 1958. New York, Columbia University Press, 1959.

Mendilow, A. A. Time and the Novel. London, Peter Nevill, 1952.

Moody, A. D. Virginia Woolf. New York, Grove Press, 1963.

Moore, G. E. 'The Refutation of Idealism', Philosophical Studies. London, Kegan Paul, Trench, Trubner and Company, Ltd., 1948.

Morozov, Mihail M. 'The Individuation of Shakespeare's Characters through Imagery', Shakespeare Survey, 2 (Cambridge, 1949), 83–106.

Muir, Edwin. The Structure of the Novel. London, The Hogarth Press, 1928.

Munro, Thomas. 'Style in the Arts: A Method of Stylistic Aesthetics', Journal of Aesthetics and Art Criticism, V (1946), 128–58.

Murry, John Middleton. The Problem of Style. London, Oxford University Press, 1922.

Ogden, C. K., and I. A. Richards. The Meaning of Meaning. 8th ed. New York, Harcourt, Brace and World, Inc., 1946.

Ohmann, Richard M. 'Generative Grammars and the Concept of Literary Style', Word (December, 1964), 423–39.

——'Literature as Sentences', College English, XXVII (1966), 261–7.

——Shaw: The Style and the Man. Middletown, Wesleyan University Press, 1962.

Pederson, Glenn. 'Vision in To the Lighthouse', PMLA, LXXII (1958), 585–600.

Peel, Robert. 'Virginia Woolf', New Criterion (October, 1933), 78–96.

Piaget, Jean. The Language and Thought of a Child. New York, Harcourt, Brace and Company, Inc., 1926.

Pool, I. de Sola, ed. Trends in Content Analysis. Urbana, University of Illinois Press, 1959.

Rader, Melvin. A Modern Book of Aesthetics. New York, Holt, Rinehart and Winston, 1952.

Read, Herbert. The Nature of Literature. New York, Horizon Press, 1956.

Richards, I. A. Principles of Literary Criticism. New York,

and London, Kegan Paul, Trench, Trubner and Company, Ltd., 1930.

——The Philosophy of Rhetoric. New York, Oxford University Press, 1936.

Rickert, Edith. New Methods for the Study of Literature. Chicago, University of Chicago Press, 1927.

Roberts, John Hawley. ' "Vision and Design" in Virginia Woolf', *PMLA*, XLIV (1946), 835–47.

Rosenblatt, Louise M. Literature as Exploration. 2nd ed. revised. New York, Noble and Noble, Publishers, Inc., 1968.

Sanford, Fillmore H. 'Speech and Personality', *Psychological Bulletin*, XXXIX (December, 1942), 811–45.

Sapir, Edward. Language: An Introduction to the Study of Speech, New York, Harcourt, Brace and Company, Inc., 1921.

Saporta, Sol, ed. Psycholinguistics. New York, Holt, Rinehart and Winston, 1961.

Scholes, Robert, ed. Approaches to the Novel. San Francisco, Chandler Publishing Company, 1961.

Schorer, Mark. 'Fiction and the "Analogical Matrix" ', Critiques and Essays in Modern Fiction, ed. John W. Aldridge. New York, The Ronald Press Company. 1952.

——ed. Modern British Fiction: Essays in Criticism. New York, Oxford University Press, 1961.

——'Technique as Discovery', *Hudson Review*, I (Spring, 1948), 67–87.

——Josephine Miles, and Gordon McKenzie, ed. Criticism: The Foundations of Modern Literary Judgment. 2nd ed. revised. New York, Harcourt, Brace and Company, Inc., 1958.

Schwartz, J., and J. A. Rycenga, ed. The Province of Rhetoric. New York, The Ronald Press Company, 1965.

Sebeok, Thomas A., ed. Style in Language. Cambridge, Mass., The M.I.T. Press, 1960.

Simon, Irene. 'Some Aspects of Virginia Woolf's Imagery', *English Studies* (Holland), XLI (June, 1960), 180–96.

Sledd, James. A Short Introduction to English Grammar. Chicago, Scott, Foresman and Company, 1959.

Spitzer, Leo. Linguistics and Literary History, Essays in Stylistics. Princeton, Princeton University Press, 1948.

——A Method of Interpreting Literature. New York, Russell and Russell, 1949.

Spurgeon, Caroline. Shakespeare's Imagery and What It Tells Us. Cambridge, Cambridge University Press, 1935.

Steinmann, Martin, Jr. 'The Old Novel and the New', ed. Robert C. Rathburn and Martin Steinmann, Jr. From Jane Austen to Joseph Conrad. Minneapolis, University of Minnesota Press, 1958.

Struve, Gleb. 'Monologue Interieur: The Origin of the Formula and the First Statement of its Possibilities', *PMLA*, LXIX (1954), 1101–11.

Stutterheim, C. F. P. 'Modern Stylistics', *Lingua*, I (1948), 410–26; III (1952), 52–68.

Tate, Allen. 'The Post of Observation in Fiction', *Maryland Quarterly*, II (1944), 61–4.

Thakur, N. C. The Symbolism of Virginia Woolf. London and New York, Oxford University Press, 1965.

Troy, William. 'Virginia Woolf: The Poetic Method', *Symposium*, III (1932), 53–63.

——'Virginia Woolf: The Poetic Style', *Symposium*, III (1932), 153–6.

Tuve, Rosemond. Elizabethan and Metaphysical Imagery. Chicago, University of Chicago Press, 1947.

——Images and Themes in Five Poems by Milton. Cambridge, Mass., Harvard University Press, 1957.

Ullmann, Stephen. The Image in the Modern French Novel. New York, Barnes and Noble, Inc., 1960.

——Language and Style. New York, Barnes and Noble, Inc., 1964.

Van Ghent, Dorothy. The English Novel: Form and Function. New York, Rinehart and Company, 1953.

Wellek, René, and Austin Warren. Theory of Literature.

New York, Harcourt, Brace and World, Inc., 1949, 'Style and Stylistics', pp. 177–89.

Wharton, Edith. The Writing of Fiction. New York, Charles Scribner's Sons, 1925.

Woolf, Virginia. The Common Reader: First and Second Series. New York, Harcourt, Brace and Company, Inc., 1948.

Whorf, Benjamin Lee. Language, Thought, and Reality, ed. John B. Carroll. Cambridge, Mass., The M.I.T. Press, 1956.

Wimsatt, William K., Jr. The Prose Style of Samuel Johnson. New Haven, Yale University Press, 1941.

——The Verbal Icon: Studies in the Meaning of Poetry. Lexington, Ky., University of Kentucky Press, 1954. 'Verbal Style: Logical and Counterlogical', pp. 201–17.

Yule, G. Udny. The Statistical Study of Literary Vocabulary. Cambridge, Cambridge University Press, 1944.

INDEX

Abrams, Mark H., 19
Auerbach, Erich, 42, 59, 164
Austen, Jane, 30, 87

'Bankes, William', 50-2, 54-5, 72-3, 90-2, 104, 117; character, 82-6, 97, 113; linguistic analysis of, 126, 128, 130-40, 188-92; imagery of, 152-3
Barnes, Djuna, 159
Beckson, Karl, 29
Bennett, Arnold, 61
Bennett, Joan, 99
Blackstone, Bernard, 96-8
Booth, Wayne C., 16, 28, 38
'Briscoe, Lily', 44-5, 51-2, 54, 71-3, 83-4, 88, 97, 100, 104, 117, 121; as central figure, 89-93, 98, 109, 111-14, 119, 123; and artistic vision, 101-3, 106, 115, 117-18, 122-3, 140; linguistic analysis of, 126-8, 130-137, 140, 196-9; imagery of, 155-7
Brontë, Emily, 162
Brower, Reuben, 24
Brown, Roger, 19

Camus, Albert, 159
'Carmichael, Augustus', 54, 58, 66, 68-73, 87, 92-3, 102
Carroll, John B., 24-5, 133-4
Céline, Louis Ferdinand, 159

Chaucer, Geoffrey, 60
Chomsky, Noam A., 124
Conference on Style (Indiana, 1958), 18
Conrad, Joseph, 27, 35, 37

Daiches, David, 89
Defoe, Daniel, 60
Dickens, Charles, 162
Diderot, Denis, 18
'Doyle, Minta', 74-5, 83, 92, 104

Eliot, George, 162
Empson, William, 19

Faulkner, William, 27, 41, 45, 60
Fernandez, Ramon, 40
Fielding, Henry, 60
Fitzgerald, F. Scott, 24
Flaubert, Gustave, 27, 32, 110
Forster, E. M., 98, 109-110
Frank, Joseph, 111
Friedman, Norman, 16, 34, 43, 112
Fries, Charles C., 124
Frye, Northrop, 60

Galsworthy, John, 61
Ganz, Arthur, 29
Gide, André, 159

Hafley, James, 98
Hardy, Thomas, 30

219

INDEX

220